MW01414380

The Lord Spoke
Her Name

The Lord Spoke
Her Name

The Remarkable Story of
Vienna Jaques in the Restoration

BRENT M. ROGERS

DESERET BOOK

Salt Lake City, Utah

© 2025 Brent M. Rogers

All rights reserved. No part of this book may be reproduced in any form or by any means without permission in writing from the publisher, Deseret Book Company, at permissions@deseretbook.com. This work is not an official publication of The Church of Jesus Christ of Latter-day Saints. The views expressed herein are the responsibility of the author and do not necessarily represent the position of the Church or of Deseret Book Company.

Deseret Book is a registered trademark of Deseret Book Company.

Visit us at deseretbook.com

Library of Congress Cataloging-in-Publication Data
(CIP data on file)
ISBN 978-1-63993-403-4

Printed in the United States of America
1 2 3 4 5 LBC 28 27 26 25 24

*In Loving Memory
of
My Grandmother
Rebecca "Becky" Ann Spainhower Rogers
(1937–2024)*

and

*My Father
Steven Paul Rogers
(1953–2024)*

Contents

Prelude: Utah Central Depot–Salt Lake City 1
Chapter 1: Early Days in New England 6
Chapter 2: Seeking and Finding 11
Chapter 3: A Missionary 17
Chapter 4: A Donation and a Revelation 23
Chapter 5: Onward to Zion 29
Chapter 6: A Word of Comfort 38
Chapter 7: Trying Times in Missouri 46
Chapter 8: Redress 54
Chapter 9: A Witness 65
Chapter 10: The Temple 72
Chapter 11: Onward to the Rocky Mountains 82
Chapter 12: A Little Milk 90
Chapter 13: A Sealing 103
Chapter 14: A Little Trouble 109

CONTENTS

Chapter 15: Relief Society 120
Chapter 16: At the Grove 126
Chapter 17: Final Days in Salt Lake City 137
Chapter 18: Laid to Rest 143
Postlude: Salt Lake City Cemetery 148
Acknowledgments 153
Notes 157
Bibliography 183
Image Credits 193
Discussion Questions 195

PRELUDE

Utah Central Depot– Salt Lake City

Early on the morning of June 8, 1876, Vienna Jaques* awoke in her Salt Lake City home perhaps with a sense of excitement, if anxiousness, about what lay ahead of her that day. She got out of bed, dressed, and readied herself for a daylong excursion south to Provo, Utah. There a stage had been set up for a major event: to greet, celebrate, and hear from pioneers of The Church of Jesus Christ of Latter-day Saints, "the aged fathers and mothers of Israel."[1]

Vienna was about to turn eighty-nine years of age. She was a tall and thin woman who dressed respectably, if plainly. Her face, gaunt with striking eyes, revealed decades of trying experiences. She had joined the Church in its infancy forty-five years earlier. From the time of her conversion to

---

* Vienna Jaques's last name is spelled by her contemporaries as well as historians in a variety of ways, including "Jakes," "Jackaways," or "Jaquish," but often as "Jacques." In every surviving document written by Jaques in her own hand, she spelled her last name the same way: "Jaques." Vienna's own spelling will be used throughout this book. Given some of the different spellings, the pronunciation of Vienna's last name is uncertain. It may have been a common French pronunciation of "Jacques" or an anglicized pronunciation sounding more like "Jakes."

Vienna Jaques as she appeared around 1867. She sat for this photograph at the Salt Lake City studio of Edward Martin. Vienna signed her name on April 2, 1867, the day she donated the photograph to the Church Historian's Office.

that June morning, Vienna demonstrated a steadfastness to build Zion and a willingness to give her all to the Church and to her Lord and Savior.

Vienna has the distinction of being one of just two women specifically named in the revelations that comprise the Doctrine and Covenants; the other is Emma Hale Smith. Though the Lord spoke her name in revelation, Vienna Jaques was not a prominent woman in the Church. Nevertheless, her experiences and the challenges she had endured for her faith were more than worth relaying to the younger generations of Latter-day Saints. Vienna had stories to tell. She was to be one of the Provo event's featured speakers.[2]

Once she finished getting ready, she walked north from her home to South Temple Street, where she boarded a mule-pulled streetcar heading west. Looking out the window, she would have seen Brigham Young's Beehive and Lion Houses as well as the Tabernacle and the not-yet-complete temple, the city's most well-known landmarks, passing on the north side of the train. After riding the streetcar for about seven large city blocks, Vienna arrived at the Utah Central Depot on the western edge of Salt Lake City's downtown area.

She stepped gingerly off the streetcar and headed into the station. It was thronged with people heading south for the "old folks' excursion."[3] More than six hundred people clamored about the depot waiting to board the Utah Southern Railroad train. The train soon pulled into the station.

Vienna and the hundreds of other passengers boarded in an orderly fashion. As the boarding process concluded, the conductor shouted "All aboard!" and the trainmen lifted the footstools from the platform. The engine revved and the horn blared. As the train gained momentum, the rhythmic click-clack of the wheels on the track grew steady. The passengers sang along to the tune of "Auld Lang Syne" as a band played.[4] They were off.

Vienna took her seat and the train picked up steam. The committee that organized the excursion consisted of Edward Hunter, the presiding bishop of the Church, George Goddard, who served as a clerk to Hunter, and Charles R. Savage, a Salt Lake City-based photographer. These men had decorated the train and labored incessantly for the comfort and happiness of the excursionists. They brought each of the travelers, including Vienna, a cup of lemonade, a slice of cake, or another refreshment to enjoy along the journey.⁵ Vienna likely enjoyed her snack and socialized with those seated around her.

As the conversation waned, perhaps she gazed out the train window to the east, admiring the towering Wasatch Mountains, which she once traversed, and which would have still been mostly green from winter snows and spring rains with just a hint of white at their highest peaks. Knowing that she would soon address a large crowd in Provo and give them "an interesting account of some of her early experience in connection with the Church," Vienna may have drifted deep into thought reviewing the memories of her life's story and contemplating what tales she would share that day.

The train made its way toward Provo for the grand gathering to hear messages from and celebrate the aged veterans of the Church.⁶ By this time in her life, Vienna Jaques had experienced so much. She could speak at length about her conversion to the gospel of Jesus Christ. She could speak about meeting the Prophet Joseph Smith. She could hold forth on the consecration of her wealth to the Church and how it provided the funds needed to procure the land on which the Saints built the first latter-day temple. She could provide a detailed description of the horrors of the Missouri experience and the comfort she found in the letter that Joseph Smith had written her. She had witnessed the first baptism for the dead in Nauvoo and could talk about what that and other priesthood ordinances had meant and continued to mean to her. She could speak about the importance of the temple, the spiritual power of the endowment she received, and the pain of leaving the sacred structure on the bluff overlooking the Mississippi River. Any of those topics, or a combination of some of them, would have fascinated the audience.

But those experiences took place in just the first fifteen years of her Church membership. What about the next thirty years of her life? She and most of the other Saints had left Nauvoo in 1846. They made the exhausting and sometimes-deadly trek to the Salt Lake Valley. There they established yet another Zion community and developed an understanding of Zion as unity within communities that would fill North and South America and eventually the world. In the Salt Lake Valley, at the base of the Rocky Mountains, Vienna established her own home and made her own contributions to building Zion. Now, as she rode the train south to Provo, it was June 1876. So much more had happened in her life that she could share with those gathered to listen to her speak.

That day in Provo was perhaps the pinnacle of Vienna's public recognition. However, exactly what she shared with the crowd that day is unknown. Like so much about Vienna's life, the contents of her talk are elusive, lost to history. The bits and pieces of documentation that Vienna left behind or that others wrote about her during her ninety-six years of life are stitched together in the pages that follow. This history takes readers through Vienna's early life in New England, her conversion to The Church of Jesus Christ of Latter-day Saints, her variety of efforts to build Zion, her participation in temple work, and the everyday challenges of overcoming trials to hear the Lord's voice. It tells of the circumstances surrounding the time the Lord spoke her name in a canonized revelation and the events that transpired through the remainder of her remarkable life.

The Lord spoke Vienna Jaques's name. He speaks all our names if we are willing to live by faith as Vienna did and if we are willing to patiently listen.

CHAPTER 1

EARLY DAYS IN NEW ENGLAND

On June 10, 1787, Vienna Jaques was born in Beverly, Massachusetts, then a small town in Essex County and the "Birthplace of America's Navy," located just north of Salem and approximately twenty miles north and east of Boston. She was born to Henry Jaques and Lucinda Hughes. Records provide some conflicting information about Henry, though it appears he was born in the Essex County town of Newbury. Lucinda was born in Ipswich, also a town in Essex County, on May 20, 1759.[1] She was descended from the English Protestant reformer John Rogers, who had translated for and helped produce the Matthew Bible in English. Rogers's work had laid a foundation for later English-language bibles including the King James Version.[2]

Henry and Lucinda began a family together in the county they had grown up in. Both Henry and Lucinda were in their late twenties at the time of Vienna's birth. She was the oldest of the Jaques children. Vienna was followed by Sarah (born in 1793), Harriet (born in 1795), and Henry (born in 1800).[3] The Jaqueses were one of nearly 640 families and approximately 3,200 individuals residing in Beverly around the time of Vienna's birth.[4] A hilly landscape with woods of pine, oak, maple, and birch and water features including ponds, streams, and lakes, including the beautiful Wenham Lake, made Beverly an inviting place for the young family.[5] For whatever reasons, perhaps employment opportunities, it appears that the Jaques family did not remain in Beverly long. They moved around regularly in Essex County.[6]

Vienna came of age with the new American nation. A New England woman of her generation likely worked alongside her mother learning and tending to domestic responsibilities. She and her family almost certainly attended a Protestant Christian church.[7] She was in her mid-twenties when the War of 1812 rocked the United States. Though no battles were fought in the areas she lived, she would have kept up on the events in newspapers. By the time Vienna reached the age of forty-two, she had not married and decided to move. The city of Boston, Massachusetts, a day's ride south from her Essex County home, beckoned her.

Moving there in the late 1820s, she found a city growing in both size and population as the first wave of European immigration was just starting to take off. The population had swelled in the decade before Vienna arrived.[8] Boston was a place of opportunity. It provided a wonderful change of scenery. A powerful segment of the city's population had profited handsomely from the War of 1812 and infused that money into the robust and diversifying local economy. The city had long boasted a maritime trading and fishing empire with a large population of individuals skilled in the operation and management of sailing ships. Its seaports and access to the lumber in nearby forests (like those in Essex County, where Vienna grew up) provided an environment ripe for growth. This was the city Vienna would call home for four years.[9]

Boston provided Vienna with greater opportunities for economic advancement. Women's economic participation, public activities, and social visibility increased in the 1830s as new textile factories recruited young and unmarried women as their labor force. This brought many young women from the countryside into the cities to work. Single women, especially those unmarried and over eighteen, began to take control of their own labor and property.[10]

The work available for women in cities like Boston was not lucrative. Work like laundry and sewing were notoriously low paying, especially compared to the financial opportunities available to men. In fact, women received one-quarter to one-half what men earned in comparable work. Nevertheless, trades, crafts, and services were diversifying New England's agricultural base in the early decades of the nineteenth century. Despite the disparities of wages and the constraints on women in society generally, women, especially single women, could accumulate wealth. But it was arduous work.

Vienna was industrious, resolute, and thrifty—characteristics prized among the era's New Englanders.[11] Early in her life, Vienna likely learned from and worked beside her mother. From this maternal example, Vienna developed an indefatigable work ethic, self-reliance, and "strict economy."[12] Those attributes proved to be hallmarks of Jaques's character during her long life.[13]

Vienna worked herself to the bone. She also made prudent economic decisions. It appears she accumulated comfortable wealth through her diligence and frugality, and she may have also had help from family. It seems that her parents before her had accumulated financial means that they passed down to her and her sister Harriet as an inheritance, which may have provided Jaques with a firm financial footing that she built upon with property ownership and other trades. Though Jaques had a brother, who would have received most of any family inheritance, he had died.[14] Nevertheless, it was Vienna's vigorous industriousness and tenacity that enabled her to accumulate and hold on to wealth in a male-dominated economic ecosystem.

By 1829, Vienna had purchased a home at 4 Norfolk Place, a small side street just east of the Boston Common, not far from where a massacre set off the American Revolution a generation earlier.[15] Property ownership was a useful tool in society that afforded Vienna economic protections and social status. Her residence was less than a mile to the waterfront on the east and, to the northeast, the Old State House, site of colonial and early state government. She was in the heart of the burgeoning metropolis.

From her home, she advertised her services as a laundress, nurse, and midwife, the latter being a specialty that she engaged in throughout her life.[16] Women working in these professions, among others, could earn decent money, especially in midwifery. Midwifery in its broadest context, the historian Laurel Thatcher Ulrich has noted, was "one specialty in a larger neighborhood economy," and was "the most visible feature of a comprehensive and little-known system of early health care . . . a mechanism of social control, a strategy for family support, and a deeply personal calling."[17] Vienna lived among individuals in similar occupations including seamstresses, nurses, shoemakers, housekeepers, and merchants. She stitched together a good livelihood.

Before long, Vienna saw the value in earning money from the unused spaces in her home. She turned her residence into a boardinghouse in 1830, welcoming visitors, newcomers, and laborers. Such an enterprise would have been demanding, adding considerably to Vienna's daily labors, but would have also brought an infusion of cash. Some boarders, male and female, stayed long enough to call 4 Norfolk Place home. With its growing population and its spate of transient workers going to and from the factories and the ports, Boston was a promising place to run a profitable boardinghouse.[18]

The enterprising Jaques had done so well in her various endeavors and had been so frugal that she had accumulated enough means to purchase and keep another residence in Providence, Rhode Island, just over fifty miles southeast from Boston, where some of her family members resided.

In both those cities, Boston and Providence, Jaques navigated challenging situations associated with being an entrepreneur and a single woman. In both those cities Jaques established relationships and built networks full of friends and family. She was a node of commercial exchange, working different jobs simultaneously to earn a living and accumulate bountiful savings. She would soon become a node of religious exchange as well.

CHAPTER 2

———

Seeking and Finding

Vienna Jaques was a spiritual seeker. During her residence in Boston, she found a spiritual home at the Bromfield Street Methodist Episcopal Church. There was a wide variety of Protestant denominations to choose from in the city and even on Bromfield Street. Methodists, Baptists, Episcopalians, not to mention Unitarian, Campbellites, and Congregationalists, all had religious offerings on Bromfield Street, a narrow thoroughfare on the northeast corner of the Boston Common.

Vienna attended her Methodist church faithfully, walking in a northerly direction less than half a mile from her residence to the Methodist worship house on Bromfield Street between Washington and Tremont Streets. This religious meeting place was one of the early Methodist churches in the city, a subsidiary or branch of what became known as the Methodist Religious Society. The first Methodist society in Boston built and ran two churches, Methodist Alley, later called North Bennett Street (considered Boston North), and Bromfield (Boston South).[1]

Though a member of the Bromfield Street Methodist Episcopal Church, Jaques was often disappointed with its worship services. She found the commitment to divine healing and revelatory power at this Methodist church to be lacking for her taste. As time wore on, she felt more spiritually incomplete.[2]

Vienna began looking for a faith that fulfilled the promises of primitive Christianity. She was among the many Americans seeking after different religious traditions. She was open-minded and often entertained the religious teachings of other faiths. She may have attended a meeting at the evangelical Park Street Church, which sat just southwest from her place of worship on Bromfield. At that church, Edward Beecher, noted American theologian and brother of Harriet Beecher Stowe, served as pastor, and William Lloyd Garrison, a social reformer and journalist, made public addresses in favor of freedom, liberty, and equality. There were many religious offerings within walking distance of Vienna's Boston residence.

Sometime before summer 1831, Vienna learned of a new faith. Rumors had circulated in the eastern United States about this new religion started by a young farm boy in western New York. The young man had been led by an angel to ancient gold plates inscribed with an unknown language. He was able to translate the language into nineteenth-century English by "the gift and power of God."[3] The result was a new book of scripture.

Vienna had read something in a newspaper about the new faith and its "golden bible." Upon hearing of Joseph Smith, the modern-day prophet of God who had grown up in the "western wilds," and of the Book of Mormon, the new scripture that he brought forth, Jaques wanted to peruse a copy of the book.[4]

She procured a copy of the new religious text, a sacred record claiming to contain "the fullness of the Gospel."[5] When she received it, however, she was not immediately drawn to the book. Holding this new scripture in her hand, Vienna quickly flipped through some of its pages but did not seriously engage with the text. She did not fully comprehend the importance of the book when she first read it, and she set it aside.[6]

After a brief time passed, Vienna felt impressed to reconsider the Book of Mormon. Then she prayed. She asked God to "impress her mind in regard to its truthfulness." She felt prompted to read the book again and to read it more closely this time. As she read, her mind became "illuminated."[7]

After reading the book, she prayed again. She prayed about the claims of this prophet and this new scripture. In an answer to her seeking, Vienna Jaques then had a "vision of the Book of Mormon" after which "she was firmly convinced of its divine authenticity."[8] She was completely satisfied that the Book of Mormon was a revelation from God.[9]

Still, Vienna wanted to investigate the Church and its teachings more closely. She decided to travel to Ohio, where revelation had guided Joseph Smith to relocate the faith's headquarters for a time. She wanted to see the Church and meet its members firsthand.

Her singleness was helpful here; her independence afforded her mobility to go to Kirtland, Ohio, to evaluate her decision to choose a new faith. Given that it was deemed improper, even dangerous, for women to travel alone (especially to the West, where steamship disasters and robberies were all too common), this was a bold action. With the same determination that she used to successfully operate her businesses, Vienna Jaques departed westward despite the potential danger that lay ahead of her.

After bravely undertaking an arduous journey first by stage from Boston to Albany, New York, where she boarded a boat on the Erie Canal to Buffalo, and thence on steamboat southwest on Lake Erie, the forty-four-year-old Jaques reached Kirtland in summer 1831. For approximately six weeks, she remained in the then-small and sparsely populated town.

At the time, there was little more to the area than Newel K. Whitney's store and a few dozen homes. It had only become a Church center months earlier when Joseph Smith moved there from New York, prompted by revelation to "go to the Ohio."[10] Vienna would have witnessed Church members busily engaged in both spiritual work and the physical construction of new buildings and dwellings. Here she met for the first time a small but growing group of believers who had also received testimonies of the Book of Mormon and of a modern-day prophet.

After only a short stay, she had seen enough to remove all doubt. Jaques was baptized into the new faith on July 12, 1831, by Emer Harris, brother of Book of Mormon benefactor Martin Harris.[11] Emer Harris himself had been baptized just five months earlier by Hyrum Smith, brother to Joseph Smith. And he too had recently arrived in Kirtland. The circumstances surrounding Vienna's momentous baptism are not known. However, from that moment on, it appears that Jaques was steadfast in her faith in the restored gospel of Jesus Christ.

At some point before returning to Boston, Jaques met Joseph Smith for the first time. The Prophet had left Kirtland in June to visit Independence, Missouri, where Church members were establishing another settlement. While in Missouri, Joseph Smith received a revelation instructing the Church to build the city of Zion in Jackson County.[12] This land was to be consecrated as a place of gathering for the Saints of God. As Vienna and the Prophet conversed, perhaps Joseph Smith told the new convert about the concepts of Zion and of gathering. From that time forward, Vienna understood that this was a man with deep faith and that the faith he led was on the move. The concept of gathering immediately appealed to this woman who had also been on the move.

Vienna prepared herself to return to Boston before fall swept in. As she traveled home to the Bay State, she engaged in conversation with a newspaper reporter who asked her about her travels. A *Boston Courier* report of October 1831 provides some details about this interview and Vienna's newfound religious devotion. The report depicts a woman, almost certainly referring to Jaques, who was returning to Boston from Kirtland at the time. "She said she had made a journey all the way from Boston to Ohio," the *Courier* reporter detailed, "to investigate the subject of Mormonism, and had satisfied herself that the Mormon bible was a revelation from God, and the leaders true prophets."[13]

Vienna revealed another aspect of the new faith that set it apart from her previous church. She told the newspaper man she "believed that the Mormonites could perform miracles." When the reporter asked if she had seen "any miraculous operations, she replied that she had seen a person who was very sick suddenly restored to health." While the newspaper wrote dismissively of Jaques's newfound faith, it nevertheless spoke to her intelligence and sincerely spiritual character. Outside of her words of praise for the new religion, the paper asserted that "she conversed like a sensible, pious woman."[14]

The Portland, Maine-based *Eastern Argus* ran a similar article about a lady traveling home to Boston from Ohio. The lady was almost certainly Vienna. While on a steamboat headed northeast on Lake Erie, the reporter asked Vienna what she had found among the believers in the Book of Mormon. She said first and foremost that the new book of scripture "was a revelation of God." The Book of Mormon was received as a new revelation and another testament of Jesus Christ. It was a revelation that could be handled, shown, read from, and passed along. Its very existence, its tangibility, made its message something to be reckoned with.

Vienna also spoke of the gathering. She learned about the revealed concept of Zion at the feet of the Prophet. On her way back to her Boston abode, Vienna informed the reporter that some Church members from Ohio had already "started for the promised land in Missouri," where the faithful would prepare themselves and their hearts for the Second Coming of Jesus Christ. "We have left Babylon, and are going to Mount Zion," was how Vienna described the doctrine of gathering, according to the reporter.[15]

Vienna also described something in the new faith that she found lacking in her Methodist church back home: prophetic direction and healings. She reiterated to this reporter that the leaders of the new faith "were true prophets" and that members among them could "perform miracles." Vienna, the practicing nurse and midwife, told of an ill person who was suddenly healed after receiving a blessing. Healings had a profound impact on Vienna. This reporter, like the writer from the *Boston Courier*, described the woman as respectable and intelligent on other topics, suggesting that Mormonism overshadowed the intellect and could lead good, smart people into superstition, something that was to be feared as distinct from true religion.[16] This would not be the last time Vienna would be ridiculed for her newfound faith. In fact, it may have been one of the milder insults she endured for it.

On her journey home to Boston, Vienna Jaques stated "that she was a Methodist when she left," but was returning a member of the new Church of Jesus Christ.[17] From Kirtland, she brought with her many copies of the Book of Mormon. Having traveled roughly 1,300 miles, she was now eager to pull those copies from her bags and distribute them to her family, friends, boardinghouse guests, patients, and acquaintances on the Atlantic coast. She took some of those copies to her second home in Providence to widen her ability to distribute the book and its message. Her work in fall 1831 through spring 1832 laid the groundwork for proselytizing activities that would soon take place in both Boston and Providence. Her missionary work prepared the way for the spread of the restored gospel in two New England cities.

CHAPTER 3

A MISSIONARY

Vienna returned to Boston—the first known convert to the restored gospel in that city.[1] She began sharing her newfound faith and its keystone text, the Book of Mormon. She was a missionary for her Church. In the summer of 1832, she assisted Samuel H. Smith (the younger brother of Joseph Smith) and Orson Hyde in their proselytizing work in the Boston area and near the location of her second home in Providence.[2]

In the eighteen months since the Church's founding, revelations instructed Church leaders to organize concerted missionary efforts to share the message of the Book of Mormon and the new faith. A January 1832 revelation instructed Smith and Hyde, as well as other missionaries, to travel to "the eastern countries" and preach to the people along the Atlantic seaboard.[3] Of this missionary effort, Hyde later stated, "This was one of the most arduous and toilsome missions ever performed in the Church." They traveled from Kirtland, Ohio, on foot along the southeastern shoreline of Lake Erie. They stopped in Westfield, New York, before proceeding to Spafford, New York, where they added fourteen members to a small branch of the Church already functioning there. Smith and Hyde traveled the length of the Empire State, entered Massachusetts, and eventually reached the capital city of Boston right on the Atlantic coastline.[4]

Though not credited by name, Vienna Jaques played a significant role in the establishment of the Boston branch. Of those approximately twenty-five new converts in Boston, the majority were women.[5] Vienna was at the center of spreading the Latter-day Saint gospel to friends, family, and acquaintances in Boston. She "spread the good news" as a forerunner to the presence of Hyde and Smith's preaching and was foundational in what became a "lively branch of the Church."[6] According to one Boston area newspaper, "Mormonite preachers have recently visited this city, and made about 15 converts to their strange doctrines, who have been baptised and joined the Mormon church."[7] They would hold regular meetings together, often in boardinghouses like Vienna's or the Myrtle Street home of another convert, Polly Vose.[8] From their homes or boardinghouses they had the opportunity to visit with neighbors or tenants and share the message of the gospel. These women facilitated the growth of the faith at a crucial time by providing shelter, finances, and speaking spaces for the early missionaries in the region.[9] This primarily female branch of the Church was created in large part due to Vienna's faith and missionary work. She exercised her religious and social power as she informed others about the gospel, transmitted its message, circulated copies of the Book of Mormon, and influenced others through her faith, actions, and example. Because of Vienna's efforts, missionaries Orson Hyde and Samuel Smith found many souls ready to embrace Christ's restored gospel.

From Boston, Hyde and Smith went to Bradford, Massachusetts, then to Saco and Farmington, Maine, before returning to the Bay State and Boston by way of Lowell. After this second stopover in Boston, the missionaries went to Providence, Rhode Island. While there, they "baptized some ten or fifteen persons amid most violent opposition." Hyde explained, "We had to flee in the night, sleep under the fence and under an apple tree."[10] Again, Vienna Jaques was instrumental in these missionary efforts. She aided them and their preaching efforts despite the fierce hostility they faced.

Jaques remained indefatigable in her efforts to preach and invite. She connected Smith and Hyde to her personal network of friends, family, and acquaintances, giving the men a constant audience for their preaching.[11] For example, Samuel Smith's diary states that on July 13, 1832, the men arrived in Providence, where they found "some of the people were believing" after they "had heard Sister Viena tell concerning the Book. Some of them came in the same evening and we taught them."[12] While there, the missionaries lodged at Jaques's second home in the Fox Point neighborhood—a location near the transportation and commerce hub on the eastside of Providence. They had "found friends" in the otherwise unwelcoming city thanks in large part to Vienna.[13] With neither purse nor scrip these two missionaries relied on Vienna for room, board, and contacts.

She testified of her faith and taught many in the Boston and Providence areas about the Church—including, especially, her family members.[14] Vienna explained Christ's restored gospel in a way that helped bring her beloved mother, Lucinda into the new faith. Sharing her sure witness with loved ones was some of the most vital missionary work she could do.

While the two missionaries were in the Providence area, Vienna also introduced them to her sister, Harriet Jaques Angell. In this religiously fluid era, Latter-day Saint doctrines offered hope to some in difficult situations. One of the doctrines that appealed to both Vienna and her sister was the idea of Zion and gathering with a righteous people to build a city of God. According to one newspaper, "Two preachers of this sect have lately visited Boston, and soon made 15 converts to their strange doctrines – some of whom are respectable persons – 5 also had joined at Lynn. Certain of these converts have cast considerable sums of money into the stock, and all were about to depart for the 'promised land,' in Jackson county, Missouri – the precious spot having been lately discovered."[15] The newspaper report referred to the concept of Zion, an ideal society patterned after the biblical city of Enoch, a community of believers living according to the principles of righteousness, harmony, and equality and preparing for the Second Coming of Jesus Christ. Faithful Church members arriving in Independence could receive an inheritance in Zion, or a plot of land on which they would reside as they helped build the united community.[16] Zion was viewed as a true place of refuge by both Vienna and her sister, Harriet.

Harriet Angell had married an abusive man named William Angell, who physically harmed her and took advantage of her plentiful financial resources. At that time, by law, women's property became subsumed under their husband when they married—and William exploited this to his benefit. Women were bound to the men they married by law.[17] "This man," Vienna said of William, had "used fraud" to marry her sister "because of her money." Together Harriet and William had one child, George Albert, who was ten years old. Vienna worried that William's "morals was so corrupt" that George Albert would be ruined if he was brought up under his father's tutelage. Vienna also feared for the safety of both her nephew and her sister. She told Samuel Smith that Harriet "was almost in danger of her life" by living with her abuser.[18] Vienna wanted a safe place for her kin. Zion, she believed, was that place.

After Samuel Smith and Orson Hyde taught Harriet about the doctrine of gathering to Zion, she informed the missionaries "that she had concluded to go to Zion . . . and thus she would get away before her husband would know anything about it."[19] She was determined to leave the

East Coast with George Albert to go to Jackson County. But her husband discovered Harriet's decision and "became outrageously angry" against the Latter-day Saint proselytizers and "said we were going to separate man and wife, and swore bitterly." Smith wrote in his diary, "I believe he would have killed us if he could."[20] Though Smith and Hyde had initially counseled Harriet to stay with her husband, they went to Jaques after this incident and "told her the things that had transpired and how hard her brother-in-law was and that she had best to take Harriet with her to Zion."[21] Vienna aided Harriet's resolve to run away to escape the abusive situation. Harriet would acquire a new community and a new identity by running away to the Saints. No longer physically bound to an abusive man who exploited her finances, Harriet could become an active partner in building the Lord's kingdom on the earth. Vienna provided spiritual and physical assistance to help her sister and nephew to the place of promised refuge.

Beyond that, Harriet Angell's story is largely unknown, except that it appears that she was baptized into the Church and that she went with her son to Jackson County, Missouri, by the fall of 1832.[22] Angell's husband had sent his brother after the child, but was rebuffed in that attempt when he arrived in Kirtland.[23] Perhaps the promise of escape from an abusive relationship and her belief in the restored gospel mingled in Harriet's mind, but she chose to become a Latter-day Saint with her sister and gather with the Saints.

Vienna and Harriet's stories provide meaning for individual choice when selecting a religious affiliation. Choosing a faith intent on moving and gathering together had significant social ramifications, including the potential to disrupt families or longstanding family dynamics.[24] Nevertheless, for some, the potential to escape a bad situation and find embrace in a united community was too strong to deny. Women could flee the wrath of abusive husbands and otherwise divorce themselves from traumatic scenes in hopes of finding peace and safety among the Saints. Though it could create complex social and familial conditions, conversion could also bring newfound hope to those who chose to run toward the restored gospel.[25]

By November 1832, Vienna, her sister, and her nephew left behind their lives on the East Coast and headed for the promised land. What preparations they made to make this pivotal move are lost to history. We do know that they paused briefly in Kirtland, where Vienna introduced Harriet to the Prophet Joseph Smith. Harriet and George Albert then went quickly to Missouri while Vienna took a brief sojourn in Kirtland. Joseph Smith wrote a letter to fellow Church leader William W. Phelps, who was in Missouri. The Prophet asked that Phelps "give [his] respects" to Harriet and to inform her that Vienna was well.[26] Something more was in store for Vienna in Kirtland. She intended to gather with the Saints in Missouri, but not before a momentous winter in Ohio.

CHAPTER 4

A Donation and a Revelation

Vienna settled in Kirtland in late November 1832.[1] Where she made her temporary residence is not known. Later accounts indicate that she temporarily moved into Joseph Smith's home, but Smith and his family did not yet have a home of their own.[2] They were living at Newel K. Whitney's store. She may have lodged there for a time as well.

Shortly after her arrival in Kirtland, Vienna met Joseph Smith again. She had been introduced to the Prophet after her baptism into the Church the previous summer. This second meeting was even more special. This time, the Prophet presented Jaques with a gift. It was an 1830 edition of the Book of Mormon in which he wrote a personal inscription on the first page: "Vienna Jaque[s] Book Novem 22$^{d.}$ 1832." Beneath the inscription, Jaques wrote, "The Writing above is Joseph Smith own handwriting which he wrote, the day he gave the book me Vienna Jaques on the 22^d of November 1832."[3] Vienna had given out many copies of the Book of Mormon in her efforts to spread the gospel message. But she treasured that copy, a gift from the Prophet, and kept it with her the rest of her life.

Vienna arrived in Kirtland at an exciting time. A revelation given in

Copy of the Book of Mormon owned by Vienna Jaques. Joseph Smith gifted this copy of the 1830 edition of the Book of Mormon to Vienna on November 22, 1832, in Kirtland, Ohio. Both Joseph's and Vienna's handwriting appear on this page, inside the book's front cover. This was a precious gift that Vienna kept from the moment she received it from the Prophet's hand.

December 1832 directed Church members to "establish a house, even a house of prayer, a house of fasting, a house of faith, a house of learning, a house of glory, a house of order, a house of God."[4] Church members learned that it would be in this House of God that they would be endowed with power as they had been told nearly two years earlier.[5] On January 11, 1833, Joseph Smith stressed the urgency of building the house in a letter to Church leader William W. Phelps, who was then living in Jackson County, Missouri. Joseph stated, "You will see that the Lord commanded us in Kirtland to build an house of God, & establish a school for the Prophets, this is the word of the Lord to us, & we must—yea the Lord helping us we will obey, as on conditions of our obedience, he has promised us great things, yea even a visit from the heavens to honor us with his own presence."[6] Though Joseph seemed to understand the importance and urgency of building the sacred structure, no progress was being made. The Church needed capital to purchase land on which to build the Lord's house and to purchase materials to construct it. Vienna Jaques had the means to help.

Before she departed from New England, Vienna appears to have liquidated at least some, if not all, of her assets, bringing with her to Ohio a significant amount of cash. During the time of her stay in Kirtland, Joseph Smith dictated a revelation on March 8, 1833, regarding particulars of Church administration, a portion of which mentioned Vienna by name. The revelation (now canonized as Doctrine and Covenants section 90) declared the will of the Lord that Vienna should receive money to gather to Zion and she would receive an inheritance in the "land of Zion."[7] By the time of the March 8, 1833, revelation, Jaques had given to the Church a substantial financial offering. During her forty-five years of life to that point, Vienna had labored diligently and saved scrupulously, accumulating wealth and properties. She decided to consecrate her means for her faith. That the Lord spoke her name and called her to go onward to Zion would have been worth all the money in the world to Vienna.

Some writers have suggested that the revelation instructed Vienna to give her money to the Church. However, it appears that Jaques gave of her money freely and that the revelation responded to that offering.[8] The March 8 revelation's language indicates that she had already given the money, stating that Jaques should receive money to bear her expenses to go to Zion, presumably some of the money she had already given, and that the residue of the money donated would be consecrated unto the

Lord. Later sources also suggest that Jaques made her donation prior to the revelation. For example, Edward Tullidge noted, "When she arrived in Kirtland she donated all of her property to the church." Furthermore, her obituary in the *Woman's Exponent* stated that Jaques's "liberality rendered such pecuniary assistance to the Church in its infancy that it called" for the March 8, 1833, revelation in which the Lord spoke her name.[9]

The precise amount of money that Jaques donated is uncertain, though several later histories state that it was around $1,400 (equivalent to approximately $50,000 in 2023).[10] While the $1,400 figure is certainly possible, no other contemporary accounts or reminiscent evidence corroborate the number. One contemporary newspaper offers a possibility. The *American Traveller* reported in August 1832 that two Latter-day Saint women from Boston had left for the "promised land," having taken with them all their wealth. According to the newspaper, these two women "had acquired by industry, one 1500 and the other 800 dollars, which they have given up to go into the general stock" of the Church.[11] The article did not name these women, but one of them may have been Vienna. (If it was Vienna, the other woman travelling with her may have been her sister Harriet). Later accounts simply note that Jaques had been "very wealthy" and that she donated all her wealth to the Church when she arrived in Kirtland.[12] Regardless of the specific number, having substantial liquid capital would have been rare at that time in an economy that was based less in cash and more in land and physical assets.

Whatever the amount, Vienna's consecration came at an advantageous time. In March 1833, Church leaders were in the midst of contracting to purchase several parcels of land in Kirtland, including the Peter French Farm. The Church needed additional funds to finalize these agreements.[13] The infusion of cash brought and donated by Vienna helped. Jaques's contribution, as Joseph Smith wrote in a later letter, "proved a Savior of life as pertaining to [the Church's] pecunary concern."[14] Her donation helped Church leaders purchase the very land on which the Kirtland Temple would be built. Her donation propelled forward progress on this sacred building project.

Vienna Jaques's economic role in the early Church cannot be overstated. While she engaged in what may have been considered traditional women's work to build her wealth, Jaques contributed financially in a way that was more typically expected of a man, only outdone by men such as Martin Harris, John Tanner, and Artemus Millett. Vienna was certainly not the only woman to have donated precious funds to the Church. For instance, Eliza R. Snow donated an unspecified amount of "cash" that was "very much needed" toward the building of the Kirtland Temple, receiving the deed to a "valuable city lot" in return.[15] Of her significant contribution to the construction of the Kirtland Temple, Eliza later said, "This, like many other trivial events in human life, proved to be one of the little hinges on which events of immense weight occasionally turn."[16] At a time when women's roles were primarily relegated to domestic duties and their religious, economic, political, and legal status and rights were largely restricted by men, the financial offerings made by these women challenge a simple reading, which would suggest the era's economic contributions to the early Church came predominantly from men.[17] Vienna, Eliza, and others demonstrated their commitment to faith by donating their means to bolster construction of the first temple in the latter-day dispensation. They helped usher in the building, which was later dedicated in a special event, all of which added to the unfolding of a process for heavenly work. Vienna's contribution, like Eliza's, indeed carried immense weight.

Vienna participated prominently in the economic arena when she contributed financially to a degree that few Church members of the time could match. She had contributed her spiritual power and connected missionaries to her relationship networks in Boston and Providence to increase the Church's membership. Now she had contributed her accumulated means, the power of financial capital, to the growing Church. She proved the literal value of women, and not just for their intimate or reproductive abilities. The revelation Joseph Smith dictated on March 8, 1833, recognized, and legitimized, her incredible contributions.

Church members would soon build the first temple of this dispensation in Kirtland on land purchased with Vienna's assistance. It would take them about three years to do so, but the spiritual keys restored because of their efforts would last generations. The restored keys opened the door for new doctrine and ordinance work, including the inception of baptisms for the dead, a teaching and practice that would deeply influence Vienna's life.

Vienna Jaques was no longer in Kirtland when the temple was being constructed or completed. She did not experience the marvelous and miraculous events that occurred. In time she would learn of and understand them, and they would have an indelible imprint on her future. In the meantime, she followed revelatory counsel and prepared for her journey to Zion.

CHAPTER 5

ONWARD TO ZION

The March 8, 1833, revelation (now canonized as Doctrine and Covenants section 90) instructed Vienna Jaques to go to "the land of Zion." Vienna had proven willing to live by the law of consecration and had donated her means to the Church. Now revelation dictated that she should "receive money to bear her expenses" to travel to Missouri. The "residue of the money" she had donated would be used for the Lord's purposes, namely the building of the Kirtland Temple. The faithful Jaques was to "receive an inheritance from the hand of the bishop" in Jackson County, Missouri.[1] That bishop was Edward Partridge. The revelation also gave Jaques a promise for the future. She would be "rewarded in mine own due time," the revelation declared, and be able to "settle down in peace in as much as she is faithful and not be idle from thenceforth."[2] What a stunning promise from the Lord through the mouth of the Prophet.

Vienna Jaques spent the months of March and April 1833 in Kirtland. While there, she likely got to know her fellow disciples better, worked industriously (as was in her nature), attended Church gatherings, and heard religious instruction from the Prophet. She also prepared to move to Jackson County on the western edge of Missouri, near the border of the organized United States of America. By the end of April, she was ready to go.

On April 30, however, a midweek meeting of the Church's high priests convened in the schoolroom of Newel K. Whitney's store altered Vienna Jaques's travel plans. Joseph Smith opened the meeting with a word of prayer, and then the men began to discuss a variety of business items. Among these topics was Jaques's "Journy to Zion." It is not known if Jaques was in attendance or was consulted on the matter, but she probably was not. Nevertheless, the Kirtland high priests decided that she should "not immediately procede" to Jackson County. Instead, she should wait an unspecified amount of time until Church member William Hobert was ready.[3] Hobert was moving to Missouri to work as a typographer for the Church's newspaper *The Evening and the Morning Star*, which was published in Independence, Jackson County, Missouri.[4] The council of high priests thought it would be best for Jaques to make the difficult, more than eight-hundred-mile trek, in company with Hobert.[5] How the council notified Jaques is not known, but she apparently followed their direction. Vienna was likely anxious to head west, but obediently waited for Hobert.

Vienna and William likely departed from Kirtland by mid-May 1833. The two traveled south and west, likely by a combination of horse and carriage, steamboat, and foot, arriving in Independence by June 7, 1833.[6] The journey between the two Church centers took about three to five weeks on average. There appears to have been some inspiration behind the decision of the high priests to have Vienna and William travel together. On the journey, Vienna put her nursing skills to great use. She experienced considerable hardship as she traveled and simultaneously cared for William, who "was afflicted with a delirium, which for a short time entirely deprived him of his natural intellect."[7] That would only be the beginning of the adversity she would face. The two beleaguered Church members limped into Zion exhausted, but safe.

Shortly after Vienna Jaques and William Hobert arrived in Independence, Church leaders there wrote to Joseph Smith and other leaders in Kirtland. Among other news items and questions, the Missouri officials told of the safe arrival of Vienna and William. This news caused Joseph and his colleagues to rejoice greatly and "thank our heavenly father that their lives have been spared till their arrival."[8]

What Vienna found when she arrived in Independence was a community of some 1,200 Church members building Zion, not yet knowing that their community would soon plunge into chaos.[9] Among the industrious efforts of Church members there in western Missouri was the Church's printing establishment. William W. Phelps, a member of the Church who had converted about the same time as Vienna in the summer of 1831, had a decade of experience in publishing, having printed and edited newspapers in western New York since 1820. Shortly after his baptism, he was appointed by revelation to be the Church's printer.[10]

Joseph Smith wanted the revelations he had received and that were guiding the Church to be made widely available to both Church members and potential converts. By the end of 1831 the Lord, through revelation, approved the compiling of the revelations into a book for distribution.[11] This book would be known as the Book of Commandments.

Oliver Cowdery and John Whitmer took manuscript copies of the revelations to Missouri where Phelps was establishing the Church's printing office where he, his wife Sally, and their four children were also living. In 1832, Phelps began the demanding task of setting the type and printing the pages that would compose that book of revelations. In addition, he edited and published a monthly newspaper for the Church titled *The Evening and the Morning Star* to provide news and information about the Church and its members.

While the Saints continued to arrive in the Independence area, there were other Jackson County residents who had already lived there for a decade. These people viewed the Church with contempt, calling it a "pretended religious sect." Among the points of contention between Church members and their neighbors was the idea and location of Zion. Church members had openly declared "that their God has given them this County of land," a sentiment that understandably did not sit well with the other residents of the county.[12]

Their holy city and the appeal of Zion was a joy and, for many like Vienna Jaques and her sister, something to run toward. The same idea was something to fear by others who believed that Church members would drive off the old settlers.[13] Sooner or later, these residents worried, the Church "must and will have the possession of our lands" in order to build their city.[14] The old settlers knew all too well what large populations of new people meant for existing populations. They had, within the previous generation, colonized land which Osage, Kickapoo, Kansa, Potawatomi, Sac and Fox, and other Indigenous nations had once called home.[15] These old settlers understood that even if Latter-day Saints did not obtain all of the lands of the county, the population growth of church members would easily tip the economic and political balance in their favor.[16] The prospect of church members possessing the entire county, whether literally all of the lands or being able to control its economy and government, "occasioned hard feelings and excited the bitter jealousy" of the other Jackson County citizens.[17]

Such sentiments about the Saints displacing old settlers and all outside their faith angered many local residents and further motivated them to oppose Church members, though it was the slavery issue that turned those motivations into violent action in July 1833.[18] At the time, Missouri was a slave state and many Jackson County citizens enslaved Black people. These enslavers did everything in their power to maintain slavery as a way of life. Those enslavers and county leaders in Jackson County mistook an editorial published in the Church newspaper's July 1833 issue titled "Free People of Color" as an open invitation from the Church to free Black people to come and settle in western Missouri. Though such an invitation was not made (the article instead encouraged Church members, especially Black members, to be cautious coming to Zion), Jackson County residents claimed that the invitation "would be to us entirely unsupportable and one of the surest means of driving us from the County."[19] These individuals were incensed, believing that Church members sought to inflict harm on enslavers in the area by encouraging free people of color to settle in western Missouri and instigate enslaved peoples there to rebellion and bloodshed.[20] This supposed invitation was the last straw.

By July 18, 1833, some Jackson County citizens had assembled themselves for riotous activities. They had been vandalizing the properties of Church members, hoping to drive them from the area. Church members, they thought, were no longer welcome in the county. On that July date, residents of Jackson County circulated a document enumerating their grievances against the Church and its members. That manifesto, signed by some three hundred Jackson County residents, stated their determination to remain on their lands and to protect their way of life by evicting Church members from the county. Two days later, on July 20, about five hundred people met at the courthouse in Independence declaring their intention to prevent more Church members from moving to the county. Those five hundred also determined to obtain "a definite pledge" from Church members that they would "remove out of the county." As long as Church members acquiesced to leave within a reasonable time, they would "remain unmolested," the citizens declared.[21]

A committee representing these hundreds of Jackson County citizens was appointed to present their agreed-upon demands to a group of Church leaders led by Bishop Edward Partridge. The bishop went to the courthouse square that day to meet the citizens' committee. The committee presented its ultimatum to him, giving him only fifteen minutes to reply. Without the ability to confer with Joseph Smith and unsure how such an agreement would jeopardize plans for the city of Zion, Partridge, in consultation with other Missouri Church leaders, declined to comply. The committee hastily returned to the courthouse, where those hundreds of Jackson County residents who had gathered were angry that Church leaders refused to leave the county. The Jackson County residents voted to demolish the Church's print shop and to attack Church members. They sprang into action.

In a chaotic scene that unfolded quickly, Jackson County vigilantes rushed to William W. Phelps's printing office and home. Some stormed inside, sending all those living there, including Sally, her infant James, and other young children running for their lives. The mobbers threw the Phelpses' belongings out the door.[22] They went upstairs, destroyed the type, and threw printing equipment out the window. They grabbed arms full of the unbound pages of the Book of Commandments, scattering them in the dusty road. Some worked to demolish the building itself by pulling apart the roof. Others pulled down the walls. In short order, these men left the Church's printing office in rubble and attempted to destroy the revelations.

Edward Partridge had returned home after his meeting at the courthouse square. As others attacked the printing office, vigilantes charged into the bishop's home. They forcibly removed him and dragged him about half a mile to the northwest corner of the courthouse square. They

Mobbers raiding the printing office in Jackson County. This artistic rendering shows the chaotic scene Vienna Jaques witnessed on July 20, 1833.

brought another Latter-day Saint named Charles Allen to the same place. Surrounded by hundreds of onlookers, some mobbers began stripping Partridge and Allen of their clothing. The bishop mustered the strength to speak: "I told them that the Saints had had to suffer persecution in all ages of the world; that I had done nothing which ought to offend anyone; that if they abused me, they would abuse an innocent person; that I was willing to suffer for the sake of Christ." The vigilantes then smeared thick, hot, sticky tar from head to foot and dumped "a quantity of feathers" on Edward and Charles. In the late colonial and early republic periods of American history, the tarring and feathering of a person was a common form of public violence meant as an outward display of criticism, humiliation, or punishment for persons deemed dangerous or unwanted in a community.²³ Edward knew he and his fellow believers had done nothing wrong, and he was willing to suffer for his faith.²⁴

Vienna Jaques had been in the Independence area of Jackson County for just about six weeks when these violent actions erupted on July 20, 1833. The details of Vienna's life during those six weeks are not known. Her experience that furious day, however, survives in the historical record. During the bedlam, perhaps to observe the commotion, Jaques gravitated toward Phelps's home and the printing office. Seeing the pages of God's revelations being trampled on and rustling about, she ran to preserve them. She got down on her hands and knees, furiously collecting as many pages as she could. As she knelt in the dirt road alone, a mobber hovered menacingly over her. The man startled the lone woman, catching her attention. He warned with a sneer, "Madam this is only a prelude to what you have to suffer."²⁵ Vienna Jaques had donated nearly all her temporal means to the Church and had moved to Missouri in anticipation of living in peace in Zion, and within weeks of her arrival, such a situation must have seemed doubtful. But even amid such trying circumstances, hope was not far away.²⁶

The intimidating man then mockingly pointed out the tarred and feathered Edward Partridge. Vienna looked up and saw the bishop walking away from the courthouse square, covered in tar and feathers. As she caught a glimpse of the abused man, she saw something miraculous. She saw her bishop "encircled in a bright light, surpassing the brightness of the sun." She was uplifted in that moment, exclaiming to herself, "Glory to God! For he will receive a crown of glory for tar and feathers."²⁷ Partridge himself later recalled: "I bore my abuse with so much resignation and meekness. . . . I was so filled with the Spirit and love of God, that I had no hatred toward my persecutors or anyone else."²⁸ As Vienna observed Bishop Partridge, the menacing mobber departed. Alone again, she continued her work to save the revelations.

Vienna was one of a few women who acted heroically to recover the revelations. Mary Elizabeth Rollins and her sister Caroline, both teenagers at the time, had observed the mob's angry charge into the Church's printing office, which was near their home. They also witnessed the unbound pages of the Book of Commandments being littered in the road. Mary and Caroline waited until the mobbers turned their backs before they sprinted to save some of the copies of the book's pages. Some of the men caught a glimpse of Mary and Caroline as they dashed behind a building. The men yelled at them to stop, trying to prevent them from taking the pages. The girls ran through a gap in a wooden fence and into a nearby cornfield, which had stalks over six feet high. They found a place to hide. They laid on top of the papers to shield the pages of revelation. Mobbers came to find the two girls and the copies but could not locate them in the massive field. Mary and Caroline were able to preserve the pages in the face of an intensely violent and harrowing situation, just like Vienna had.[29]

The Jackson County citizens had taken matters into their own hands, using violent action as a means of control. After they had completed their destruction, they gave notice that they would return in three days to see if Partridge and the other Church members would reconsider the decision to remain in their homes and continue to build Zion in Jackson County.[30] After experiencing the fury of July 20, Partridge and other Church leaders signed a "memorandum of the agreement" on July 23, 1833, promising that Church members would leave Jackson County—half of them by January 1, 1834, and the other half by April 1, 1834.[31] They did so for the safety of their people. Yet they remained committed to the "Holy Land" of Zion.[32] Safe for the moment, Vienna cried alone, knowing that she would be on the move again. Though in the place designated as the promised land, Zion felt so far away.

CHAPTER 6

A Word of Comfort

Vienna had written a letter to Joseph Smith sometime after her arrival in Independence, Missouri. Her letter, which included "a history of [her] Journey" and a notification of her "safe arrival," has not been found. Precisely when Joseph Smith received that letter is also unknown. It had made its way to Smith some time before September 4, 1833, when he wrote to her in reply.

Other news from Missouri had also reached him. By August 10, he heard about the violent acts of Missourians against members of the Church and by August 18, he had received even more information that left him in despair. He prayed earnestly for answers to the question of "why God hath suffered so great a calamity to come upon Zion." He prayed and prayed about the great tribulation facing the Church in Missouri but felt confused as to what should happen next. The voice of the Lord would only say to him, "Be still, and know that I am God." Among the promptings he had, Joseph Smith discouraged Church members and leaders from giving up their lands in Jackson County despite the agreement that had been made for them to leave or face more violence.

"Not one foot of land perchased should be given to the enimies of God or sold to them," he told Church members in western Missouri.[1] The Prophet also felt a spiritual prompting to write a letter directly and specifically to Vienna Jaques.

Smith spoke the words he wished to say to Vienna as a scribe penned them. "Having a few Leisur moments I sit down to communicate to you a few words," the letter began, "if it should be a satisfaction for you to receive a few words from your unworthy brother in Christ."

During such a trying time, Vienna, a woman of remarkable faith, surely would have been kneeling in frequent supplication to the Lord. She had written to a prophet of God searching for answers and relief. Ever since Joseph received her letter, he had felt the whisperings of the Spirit telling him that Vienna had been praying for comfort, and he felt a divine obligation to communicate with her. Joseph stated that the Spirit told him, "thou art indebted to thy God for the offering of thy Sister Viana [Vienna Jaques] which proved a Savior of life as pertaining to thy pecunary concern therefor she should not be forgotten of thee for the Lord hath done this." The prompting further encouraged the Prophet to "remember her in all thy prayers and also by letter for she oftentimes calleth on the Lord saying O Lord inspire thy Servant Joseph to communicate by letter some word to thine unworthy handmaid."[2] Joseph's letter to Vienna was in direct response to the whisperings of the Spirit and an answer to Vienna's fervent prayers. She had sought words of peace from the Prophet and an assurance that all her sins were forgiven.

Knowing some of what she experienced in the July violence, Joseph addressed the situation. He told her that he had a sense "that the Lord would chasten" her when she left Kirtland in May. Such news may have taken Vienna aback. If he had such an inclination, why didn't he warn her before she left? She had been so full of hope and joy at the prospect of gathering to Zion. Joseph then told Vienna that he had "pray(ed) fervantly in the name of Jesus that you might live to receive your inheritance agreeable to the commandm[e]nt which was given concerning you," but stated "I am not at all astonished at what has happened to you neithe[r] to what has happened to Zion." Joseph did not "feel disposed to cast any reflections" but "to cry mightily unto the Lord that all things might work together for good."[3] The need to repent and follow the commandments would not have been new for the woman of faith. The hope that she would yet receive her inheritance as the Lord outlined in revelation would have given Vienna reason to cheer despite the violence and pain she had endured in Missouri to that point.

Echoing scriptural language, the Prophet said further, "I feel to say O Lord let Zion be comforted let her waste places be built up and established an hundred fold let thy saints come unto Zion out of every nation let her be exalted to the third heavens and let thy Judgments be sent forth unto victory."[4] In the weeks before Joseph dictated this letter to Vienna, he similarly encouraged Church leaders in Missouri to "be of good cheer." He hoped that his letters would "refresh the hearts and revi[v]e the spir[i]ts" of those afflicted.[5]

In his lengthy missive to Vienna, Smith wrote more words of comfort and guidance, stating, "After this great tribulation let thy blessings fall upon thy people, and let thy handmaid live till her soul shall be satisfied in beholding the glory of Zion, notwithstanding her present affliction she shall yet arise and put on her beautiful garments and be the Joy and glory of the whole earth, therefore let your heart be comforted, live in strict obedience to the commandments of God and walk humble before him and he will exalt thee in his own due time."[6] Significantly, the letter not only offered thanks and comfort to Jaques but also passed along important information about Church business and the building of Zion. Vienna would have likely felt the faith of a prophet of God upon receiving the letter, but also the trust of a friend. Being the vessel through which news and information flowed, a position normally reserved for the leading men of the Church, would have let Vienna know she was an equal laborer in the Lord's vineyard.

Joseph shared news of the Church's growth and temple construction in Kirtland. He informed Vienna, "There has many brethren mooved to this place from different parts of the country so much so that one house is not sufficient to contain them for public worship." Therefore, he stated, "We have divided and hold meetings in two sepperete places namely at the school house on the flats and Uncle John Smiths who lives on brother [Joseph] Coes place." Next, he provided a monumental, though understated, announcement. "We have commenced building the house of the Lord in this place," the Prophet proclaimed, "and are making great progress in it so much so that I feel great hopes that by spring it will be finished."[7]

Construction on the temple had begun just weeks after Vienna departed Kirtland for Missouri. Hyrum Smith had started digging trenches for the foundation of the Kirtland Temple on June 7 (approximately the same day Vienna arrived in Independence). He began the work in earnest that day and by fall 1833, the stone foundation had been completed and some girders were in place to support the first floor. Joseph's hope that the temple would be completed by spring was quickly dashed, as a lack of building materials and a new priority to help relieve Church members like Vienna Jaques in Jackson County temporarily halted construction on the sacred structure.[8]

Joseph Smith's letter provided reports of missionary success in the eastern United States. He told of David W. Patten raising a branch of the Church in New York with eighty-three members. Joseph relayed to

Vienna the miracles of Patten's ministry: "Many were healed through his instrumantality several [physically disabled people] were restored as many as twelve that were afflicted came at a time from a distanc[e] to be healed he ⟨and others⟩ administered in the name of Jesus and they were made whole." Joseph perhaps had sought to remind Vienna in her trials that the Lord's miracles had not ceased. "Thus you see," Joseph declared, "that the Laborers in the Lords vineyard are Labouring with their mights."[9]

The Prophet provided information for Vienna to give to Bishop Edward Partridge. "I wish you to say to brothe[r] [Edward] Partridge," Joseph stated, "that we received his lette[r] of the 13 August directed to Bro Frederick [G. Williams] requesting an explination on the Plan of the house which is to be built in Zion and also of the City Platt that ⟨the⟩ brothern whom we have recently sent to Zion will give them all the information they need about it."[10] Joseph was referring to important documents that guided the growth of Zion and the Houses of the Lord, or temples, that were to be built there. In the aftermath of the July violence, Partridge may have wondered if the plans to build Zion had changed. Joseph's instructions would make clear that the work of the Lord must move forward even in the face of adversity. Vienna would have immediately gone to Bishop Partridge, whom she had seen brutally tarred and feathered just a couple of months earlier, to share the news. The plan for Zion and temple building would not cease.

In mid-August, Joseph Smith had the plans for the city of Zion and its temples revised with more detailed instruction. He believed that "the day will come that Zion will be keept for our sakes therefore be of good cheer and the cloud shall pass over and the sun shall shine as clear and as fair as heaven itself and the Event shall be Glorious."[11] The presidency thus once again directed Church leaders in Missouri to commence building the House of the Lord in Jackson County despite the threats they faced. The revised city plat and modified temple design were sent to Missouri by special messengers Orson Hyde and John Gould. These special messengers arrived in Jackson County in late September 1833.[12]

Joseph's letter provided Vienna with information about some of her friends or acquaintances from Boston, which would have certainly buoyed Vienna's spirits. The letter noted that "Brothe[r] Ball and Siste[r] Elizabeth Chase arived here ⟨from⟩ boston." Joseph T. Ball had likely converted to the Church around the same time that Vienna was helping Orson Hyde and Samuel Smith teach the gospel in the Boston area. He has been identified as a Black man who was a cooper by trade and went on to become a successful missionary.[13] Elizabeth Chase was a fifty-three-year-old widow who had been baptized into the Church of Christ (as the Church was named at that time) in Boston by Samuel Smith on December 5, 1832.[14] She stayed with Joseph Smith's family during her brief sojourn in Kirtland.[15]

Joseph also mentioned that Agnes Coolbrith and Mary Bailey were residing at his father's home in Kirtland.[16] Coolbrith and Bailey were baptized in Boston after being taught by Samuel Smith and Orson Hyde during the men's 1832 mission in that area. According to Bailey's obituary, she left Boston sometime in 1833, "in company with Miss Coolbrith, . . . she bid farewell to friends and connexions, and every thing most dear, and traveled the distance of one thousand miles to Kirtland, Ohio, with no human protector but the one above named, to associate with the saints, in obedience to the commands of God, and the instructions of the inspired Prophets and Apostles." Lucy Mack Smith's history notes that in June 1833, "Mary Baily and Agnes Colby [Coolbrith] was then boarding with me they devoted their whole time to making and mending clothes for the brethren who worked on the house There was but one main spring to all our thoughts and that was building the Lords house." Coolbrith and Bailey later married Joseph Smith's brothers Don Carlos Smith and Samuel Smith, respectively.[17] Learning comforting news about individuals from home certainly would have been a balm to Vienna's soul.

Finally, Joseph's letter ensured that Vienna understood that neither she nor her donation had been forgotten. He said, "I will assure you that the Lord has respect unto the offering you made he is a God that changes not and his word cannot fail remember what he has said in the book of mormon respecting those who should assist in bringing this work forth." The Prophet may have been referring to 1 Nephi 13:37: "And blessed are they who shall seek to bring forth my Zion at that day, for they shall have the gift and power of the Holy Ghost; and if they endure unto the end they shall be lifted up at the last day, and shall be saved in the everlasting kingdom of the Lamb; and whoso shall publish peace, yea, tidings of great joy, how beautiful upon the mountains shall they be." Joseph responded to the promptings he had felt and to Vienna's prayers with a letter of gratitude and comfort. Joseph closed the letter with a reminder of the work being done on the temple and that he himself was "Labouring on the house of the Lord with my own hands." He humbly signed the letter "your unworthy brother in christ."[18] The knowledge that neither the Prophet nor the Lord would forsake her in this time of extreme trial would have given Vienna more strength and courage to face her challenges.

Joseph Smith's letter to Vienna Jaques is the earliest surviving letter from Smith addressed specifically to a woman (other than his wife Emma). The letter provides a glimpse into an important moment in Church history, into the lives of people in the Church, but specifically into the lives and character of Vienna and Joseph. It provides evidence of the Prophet's egalitarian and inclusionary nature regarding women.[19] Smith trusted Jaques with information. He also reminded her that God is no respecter of persons and that He hears and answers prayers.

The letter was postmarked on September 11, 1833, and would have likely arrived in Jackson County in early October. Vienna would have felt an immense joy and uplift from its words and messages; she cherished that letter and often shared its contents with others throughout her life.[20] She would need that spiritual and emotional boost. The letter arrived just weeks before violence against the Saints in Missouri resumed.

CHAPTER 7

Trying Times in Missouri

Just over three months had passed since Vienna Jaques experienced the horrific events of July 20, 1833. Latter-day Saint leaders, under duress, had placated their non-believing Missouri neighbors by agreeing to fully vacate Jackson County by April 1834. In return, the Jackson County residents were to leave the Saints in peace. That peace, however tenuous, was short-lived. The Saints believed their constitutional rights had been violated and soon determined not to abandon their legally purchased lands as they had previously agreed. When that became apparent to other residents they were demonstrably upset. They had fully expected the Saints to depart the county.[1] "We are determined to drive you away from this Country," one Jackson County resident yelled at Latter-day Saint David Pettegrew, "and we will stop you from emigrating here."[2] As the fall weather settled into western Missouri, Jaques and the Saints again became embroiled in violent conflict in Jackson County.

For his part, Joseph Smith advised Church members to neither sell nor abandon their lands in Jackson County. Instead, in a letter written on August 18, 1833, the Prophet encouraged them to "send Embasadors to the authorities of the government and sue for protection and redress."[3] Early in October 1833, Church leaders Orson Hyde and William W. Phelps traveled to Jefferson City, Missouri, and delivered a petition to Missouri governor Daniel Dunklin, asking him to raise troops to protect the Church members so they could defend their homes and rights and initiate lawsuits for "the loss of property—for abuse—for defamation."[4] The Missouri Church leaders also suggested that the perpetrators of the violence against them be tried for their crimes.

Joseph's August 1833 letter foreshadowed events to come. He testified that he knew the Lord would "spedily deliver Zion" and he expressed hope that God would spare his life and allow him to settle on an inheritance in the "land of Zion in due time." He also stated that Church leaders in Kirtland would "wait the Comand of God to do whatever he please and if he shall say go up to Zion and defend thy Brotheren by the sword we fly."[5] The Prophet's letter likely provided hope to Church members in Missouri that Zion would still be realized in Jackson County.[6]

But the governor would not help protect the Saints. So, Church members took it upon themselves, publicly declaring their intentions to defend themselves and to remain on their lands. This was, after all, their land of promise, a place that had been "dedicated unto the Lord forever" and land that they had legally purchased.[7] Church leaders also hired legal counsel. These actions angered their opponents, who began to organize again on October 21. Within a week they had "voted to a hand to move the 'mormons.'"[8] As their opponents mobilized, Church leaders gave members strict orders "not to be the aggressors—but to warn them not to come upon us." For members like Vienna Jaques, "It was a solemn looking time."[9] As October came to a close, the spark was ignited and violence against the Saints resumed.

On October 31, "a mob of forty or fifty, collected and proceeded armed to a branch of the church, who lived eight or ten miles south west of Independence, there they unroofed ten houses, and partly threw down the bodies of some of them; they caught three or four of the men, and notwithstanding the cries, and entreaties of their wives and children, they whiped, and beat them in a barbarous manner."[10] Over the next several days, the simmering tension boiled over into armed conflict. On November 4, a battle occurred between the Saints and their opponents near the Big Blue River resulting in a few injuries and deaths.[11]

Believing that fighting over their refusal to vacate Zion would continue indefinitely, Missouri Church leaders met during the night of November 4, 1833, to discuss future movements. Upon "seeing the rage of the people," and on the advice of Lieutenant Governor Lilburn W. Boggs, they determined that it was best for the Church and its members to leave Jackson County immediately "rather than to have so many lives lost as probably would be."[12] On November 5, 1833, Colonel Thomas Pitcher, acting without official authorization, called out the Missouri militia to restore peace in the area. Pitcher and his troops forced nearly 150 Church members to surrender their arms and weapons and had several Latter-day Saint men imprisoned.[13] With the militia and mobs actively pursuing them, men, women, and children of the Latter-day faith fled in all directions from their promised land. By November 7, the shores of the Missouri River "began to be lined on both sides of the ferry, with men, women, children, goods, waggons, boxes, chests, provisions, &c."[14] By mid-November, nearly all members of the Church had retreated from Jackson County, leaving their lands and most of their other property behind. A group of some one hundred women and children wandered on the prairies of western Missouri for days without food or shelter.[15]

The Saints in Missouri became refugees in neighboring counties, primarily in Clay County, struggling to survive as fall quickly turned to winter.[16] For housing, the refugees in Clay County built huts in the woods, occupied abandoned slave cabins and other vacant structures, set up tents, or lived in the open risking exposure.[17] One Church member, Emily M. Austin, later recalled the harrowing experience: "We gathered up what little we could take in wagons and crossed the Missouri river and pitched our tents in Clay county, on the bank of the river. Many were taken with chills and fever, and altogether the Mormons presented a pitiable spectacle. . . . We lived in tents until winter set in, and did our cooking out in the wind and storms. Log heaps were our parlor stoves, and the cold, wet ground our velvet carpets, and the crying of little children our piano forte; while the shivering, sick people hovered over the burning log piles here and there."[18] Jaques, like most of her fellow believers, fled and emerged a refugee in Clay County in the winter of 1833–34. Vienna and the Saints could only wait for reinforcements.

Though an October 1833 revelation noted that "Zion shall be redeemed," it was not until Joseph Smith received a revelation on December 16 and 17 that the path for that redemption was understood.[19] The mid-December revelation reiterated that Church members were not to sell their lands in Jackson County. More importantly, through the parable of the woman and the unjust judge, the revelation instructed members to, in sequence, seek for redress through the judicial system, then from the governor of Missouri, and finally from the president of the United States. The revelation also gave the parable of a nobleman and his vineyard, further indicating how members of the Church were to reclaim their lands: by gathering up the strength of the Lord's house—the young men through the middle-aged—and sending them to Zion to protect the Church there.

Similar to the instruction given in the mid-December 1833 revelation to gather resources to redeem Zion, a February 24, 1834, revelation authorized the recruitment of people and the raising of funds to support an armed expedition to help the Missouri refugees reclaim and resettle their Jackson County lands. This expedition later became known as the Camp of Israel or Zion's Camp.[20] The February 24 revelation specified that the expeditionary force should number at least one hundred, with preferably five hundred individuals. It also reminded Church members, as Joseph Smith had stated more than two months earlier, that "after much tribulation . . . commeth the blessing." This revelation was quite specific about the promised blessing: the restoration of Church members to the land of Zion.[21] That restoration was to come from the power of the Joseph Smith–led volunteer force.

By the beginning of May 1834, Joseph Smith had finalized arrangements to take the expeditionary force (then numbering around 230 men, women, and children) from Kirtland to western Missouri. They began a grueling march with the hope of returning the beleaguered Saints to their lands in Jackson County and protecting them thereafter.[22]

The Camp of Israel arrived in western Missouri by June 19. They camped near the Fishing River, a tributary of the Missouri River, some ten miles east of Liberty in Clay County. Vienna Jaques was encamped near Fishing River when Joseph Smith and the members of Zion's Camp reached that waterway. Because Governor Dunklin refused to call up the state militia to help the Saints, the camp did not deliver the Saints, nor return them to their Jackson County lands as hoped. Joseph Smith received a revelation on June 22 informing the camp's members that the Lord no longer required them to redeem Zion at that time.

Many of the Zion's Camp members became ill from cholera, a bacterial disease spread through contaminated water, while they were encamped near Fishing River. The disease struck camp members suddenly and spread quickly. Joseph B. Noble wrote of his experience with the illness: "I was violently seased . . . puking and purging powerfully then cramping from head to foot in the most powerful manner with a burning fever in my bowels."[23] Healthy camp members and other Church members exerted themselves "considerably to attend to the sick."

Vienna Jaques was among the first to aid the sick. Utilizing skills she had honed over a lifetime of healthcare service, Vienna was a productive caregiver in this moment of need. Heber C. Kimball, a participant in the Camp of Israel prior to his appointment as one of the Church's Twelve Apostles, was one of those who fell ill. Kimball remarked that he "received great kindness . . . from sister Vienna Jaques." Vienna administered to his wants and needs and provided care to a number of the other camp members.[24] She was a figure of mercy, love, and care for the participants of Zion's Camp at this time of sickness. Despite the valiant efforts of Vienna and other caregivers, thirteen camp members and two other Church members died during this cholera outbreak.

By the end of June, Zion's Camp was disbanded. After spending the better part of the first week of July instructing the Saints in Clay County, Joseph Smith and the members of Zion's Camp returned to Kirtland, leaving Vienna and the Missouri Saints to move forward on their own.

Vienna apparently remained in western Missouri for the next two years. She was not present for the completion and dedication of the Kirtland Temple, though her monetary contribution nearly three years earlier had enabled the Church to purchase the lands on which the temple was built. The dedication of the Kirtland House of the Lord on March 27, 1836, was the result of years of devoted effort and sacrifice, and it was a glorious event for those who gathered for the ceremony.[25] Joseph Smith's journal records that following the Savior, Moses, Elias, and Elijah appeared, instructed Joseph and Oliver Cowdery, and restored to them the keys "of the fullness of the Melchezedek Priesthood."[26] These keys included the authority to gather "Israel from the four parts of the Earth" and the authority "to turn the hearts of the Fathers to the children, and the children to the fathers," as had been prophesied in the Old Testament and Book of Mormon.[27] Furthermore, the restoration of those keys provided the authority to perform ordinances and sealings for eternal marriages and eternal families for both the living and the dead.

The determined effort of Church members to prepare for the dedication of the Kirtland temple reached a crescendo of jubilation and spiritual outpouring on that April day. The restoration of those priesthood keys proved to be a new beginning, an immense theological development for the Latter-day Saint faith. Though contemporary documents do not shed light on whether Joseph Smith and the Saints immediately understood the fullness of this vision, the Kirtland Temple had unlocked a new gateway for a great divine work to begin.

In spring 1836, Vienna Jaques would have been among the hundreds of Latter-day Saints living in Clay County. The growing population of Saints in the county concerned non-believing residents as it had in Jackson County three years earlier. The summer of 1836 again saw the Saints under siege as violent threats against them escalated. The Saints were again forced to leave their homes in western Missouri. This time, they fled approximately thirty miles north to a "mill seat on Shoal creek" in Caldwell County.[28] There, the Church established the settlement of Far West. Church members flocked to the area. By July 1837, the settlement's population was around fifteen hundred and would continue growing.[29] Vienna was among that number. She was soon joined by Joseph Smith, his family, and many Church leaders and members who moved there from Kirtland, Ohio.

Far West was to be a city of Zion with a temple. A Joseph Smith revelation dated April 26, 1838, had designated it as such.[30] That month also saw major changes in Church leadership. For example, longtime leaders Oliver Cowdery and David Whitmer were excommunicated while Brigham Young took on a new leadership role in the Zion presidency.[31] Joseph Smith engaged in reorganizing the leadership to strengthen the Church and its members.

Writing from Far West, Vienna likely put information about these changes in a letter she sent to her hometown in Essex County, Massachusetts. In May 1838, Latter-day Saint missionary Wilford Woodruff (who would later be both an apostle and President of the Church) was in Essex County proselytizing. There he met a "Mr. Burbanks," who had recently received a letter from Vienna in Far West. While visiting, Burbanks allowed Woodruff to peruse the letter, which Woodruff wrote about in his journal. He said simply, "It contained many important things concerning the Saints."[32] Woodruff continued to teach the gospel in Vienna's old stomping grounds in the northeastern United States, while Vienna shared information about the Church with friends and confidants there.

Vienna Jaques had already experienced so much anguish and tribulation in her years in Missouri. For five years, she had seen a vicious cycle of threats, violence, and evacuation with only moments of peace interspersed. Now she lived in Far West, and the Prophet was there. But, just as the focus of the Saints turned to building up their new city of Zion, the cycle would resume.

CHAPTER 8

REDRESS

The Latter-day Saint population in western Missouri had swelled to over twelve thousand by 1838. Just like they had in Jackson and Clay counties, the Saints built houses, cultivated farms, and operated businesses on land they had legally purchased or obtained in Caldwell and neighboring counties. And just as it had before, violence soon followed. This time, however, it escalated into war. Again, there would be no help from the government. This time the Missouri governor, Lilburn W. Boggs, issued an executive order. The Latter-day Saints were to be driven from the state or killed, it said. The governor was calling for the extermination of the Saints in Missouri. Like other Latter-day Saints, Vienna Jaques would endure the aftermath of the governor's order and the battles that broke out between Church members and their opponents.

Vienna was not present for the Hawn's Mill Massacre, a bloody attack that took place in a small Latter-day Saint settlement on October 30, 1838, but she would have been caught up in the widespread panic that grew out of that tragedy. News of the murders of seventeen Latter-day Saints by Missouri militia "caused a regular stampede" among the faithful throughout Caldwell County. Some women took their children in their arms, while other Church members hurriedly grabbed clothes, a loaf of bread, or a blanket and rushed into the snow and adjacent timber to hide.[1] On October 31, a messenger delivered news of the massacre to Joseph Smith, who was then at Far West, roughly sixteen miles west of the mill. News of the tragedy led to the Prophet's decision to surrender to the governor's militia force at Far West. In a later history of these events, John Corrill wrote that "Smith appeared to be much alarmed, and told me to beg like a dog for peace, and afterwards said he had rather go to States-prison for twenty years, or had rather die himself than have the people exterminated." Corrill continued: "Smith said if it was the Governor's order, they would submit, and the Lord would take care of them."[2] Joseph Smith would spend more than five months in Liberty Jail.

At Hawn's Mill and other sites of conflict during the so-called Mormon War, Missouri militiamen plundered the Saints' property, harassed survivors (especially women), killed livestock, and robbed the people of about "a hundred bushels of wheat and about as much corn."[3] Women were especial targets for militiamen; reports and testimonies stated that women were physically abused and even suffered sexual violence from their attackers. Latter-day Saint women were "made to suffer all the indignities that the most brutal barbarity could inflict."[4] The militia also burned all the books they could find and continually threatened to burn the Saints' homes and fields, or worse.[5] Over the next few days, Missouri authorities arrested sixty-four Church members.

Vienna's experiences and perspective during this time of war and violence were either not recorded or have not survived. But, facing the prospect of state-sanctioned death, she chose to leave the state with nearly all other Latter-day Saints. She traveled east to Illinois.

The experiences of other Latter-day Saints open a window into the difficulties shared by the faithful. A small number of Latter-day Saints left Missouri in November, but the majority did not depart until February or early March 1839, when it was decided that the main body of the Church would temporarily relocate to the town of Quincy in Adams County, Illinois. Latter-day Saints held to the hope that they would either get their property back so that they could sell it or that the government would rescind the extermination order, but neither happened.[6] In the end, most of the Saints found little or no opportunity to sell what possessions they still had. Joseph Holbrook estimated that prior to the outbreak of the Mormon War he could have sold his property for two thousand dollars but following the conflict he had "only 1 yoke of old oxen and 2 cows left."[7] The Saints were again on the move and perhaps more destitute than ever.

Amanda Smith left for Illinois on February 1, 1839, with four children under the age of twelve, including her young son Alma, whom she had nursed back to health after he was shot in the blacksmith's shop at Hawn's Mill next to his father, Warren, and brother Sardius. Warren and Sardius did not survive, leaving Amanda a widowed mother of young children. Amanda later recounted that she and her children slept outdoors all the way to Quincy, where she "found friends who took me in and supplied my wants for a season."[8] In a letter to the *Missouri Republican*, Missouri politician David R. Atchison (a major-general in the state militia and a Latter-day Saint sympathizer) commented on the exodus: "At least 200 women, nearly every one of whom has a family of small dependent children have been left without any one to provide for them, with no means of support, without shelter from the storm, without protection from the cold, or food to satisfy the cravings of appetite."[9] Without access to horses or wagons, many of the Saints walked in wintry conditions the entire way to Quincy. John Hammer, who was just nine years old at the time, vividly remembered the stark conditions of the forced exodus from Missouri. In a stirring account he recalled:

> When night approached we would hunt for a log or fallen tree and if lucky enough to find one we would build fires by the sides of it. Those who had blankets or bedding camped down near enough to enjoy the warmth of the fire, which was kept burning through the entire night. Our family, as well as many others, were almost barefooted, and some had to wrap their feet in cloths in order to keep them from freezing and protect them from the sharp points of the frozen ground. This, at best, was very imperfect protection, and often the blood from our feet marked the frozen earth. My mother and sister were the only members of our family who had shoes, and these became worn out and almost useless before we reached the then hospitable shores of Illinois. All of our family except the two youngest Austin and Julian had to walk every step of the entire distance, as our one horse was not able to haul a greater load; and that was a heavy burden for the poor animal. Everything bulky or anyway heavy was discarded before starting. Such articles as my father's cooperage tools, plows and farming implements we buried in the ground, where they may have remained undiscovered to the present time. There was scarcely a day while we were on the road that it did not either snow or rain. The nights and mornings were very cold. Considering our unsheltered and exposed condition, it is a marvel with me to this day how we endured such fatigues without being disabled by sickness, if not death.[10]

After such a harsh journey, the refugees, including Vienna Jaques, found refuge and a kind reception in Quincy. As early as February 27, 1839, public meetings were held in the community, and local merchants and other individuals donated food, clothing, money, and other items to the suffering Saints.[11] By March 17, 1839, Wilford Woodruff noted that "Quincy was full of Mormons," and the next day he and several others helped move "a number of families that had Camped on the bank of the river . . . [who] were in a suffering Condition with Cold, rain & mud & some want of food."[12] The 1,800 citizens of Quincy welcomed more than 5,000 Saints and cared for their needs.

In March 1839, Joseph Smith, still imprisoned in western Missouri, addressed a letter to the Church in Quincy instructing the Saints to seek redress in the form of aid and compensation from the federal government for the violence they suffered and their forced exodus from Missouri. They were to seek redress through written petitions and appeals.

Joseph Smith wanted the federal government and the American nation to understand the suffering of his people. He encouraged the Saints to gather together "a knowledge of all the facts and sufferings and abuses put upon them" by the state of Missouri.[13] Both Church leaders and members quickly responded to that request. By the summer of 1839, hundreds of the beleaguered Saints went before an Adams County justice of the peace and gave sworn affidavits, testimonies, and petitions that detailed their suffering and enumerated their losses. Collectively, these petitions recount the trying and brutal experiences the Latter-day Saints faced in Missouri.

The earliest events described in the petitions are those of the Saints in Jackson County in 1833 who were expelled from that county. They tell the story of the continuing trials and persecution of the Saints, culminating in the 1838 extermination order. Six hundred seventy-eight individuals (only seventy of whom were women) petitioned for redress. In addition to psychological trauma, the petitions detail many individuals' loss of land and property, amounting to thousands upon thousands of acres of land and hundreds of thousands of dollars of personal property.[14]

Vienna Jaques's name resurfaces in the historical record in connection with the production and collection of these redress petitions in 1839. Jaques, like so many other Missouri Saints, had lost property with no remuneration, but she did not give a sworn statement herself. By this time, the ever-industrious and independent Vienna Jaques had found a partner and decided to marry. Her name was included in the affidavit of her husband, as was the legal custom of the day.

The circumstances of Vienna's marriage are not known. Sometime before May 7, 1839, she married Daniel Shearer, a whip maker and blacksmith who had been jailed in Missouri during the Mormon War and who later served on a committee aiding poor Church members in their move from Missouri.[15] By this time, Vienna would have been fifty-one years old. Daniel was forty-seven and a widower with at least one son, his first wife having passed away in 1823.

On May 7, Shearer, who had relocated to Illinois with Jaques, made an affidavit recording financial losses for himself and Jaques. Since legally her identity had been assumed by her husband when they were married, Shearer requested $250 in reparations on her behalf from the government for damages "in being driven from Jackson County in the State of Missouri & Mooving from the State of Massachusetts to Missouri."[16] The $250 for Vienna was significantly less than she had when she joined the Church. Shearer placed his own claim at $1,200 for his move from New York and "for being denied Constitutional rights."[17] Shearer claimed an additional $300 for loss of lands, $500 for loss of town property, $240 in time and board, $150 for "unlawfull & false imprisonment," and another $585 for the detainment of his son. Finally, Shearer included $4.50 more for the theft of a pair of pistols taken "by a man Calling himself

Colonel Jones." Altogether Shearer petitioned the federal government for $3,129.50 for the trauma he, his son, and Vienna experienced in Missouri.[18]

Because Vienna Jaques had no legal option for recourse for herself in this matter, this appears to be one of the few times that she relied on another to voice her concerns. Though married, Vienna remained independent; she was never content to be confined by the dictates of a nineteenth-century marriage.

Vienna and the Saints quickly moved on from Quincy, Illinois. Grateful for the assistance rendered them in their time of need, Church leaders led the Saints to a small town on the east bank of the Mississippi River about fifty miles north of Quincy. This settlement was in Hancock County, Illinois. It would be named Nauvoo, a Hebrew word for a beautiful place. While still suffering the effects of violence in Missouri, and in addition to the numerous affidavits calling for redress and remuneration, many of the Saints took up pen and paper, turning the mental, emotional, and physical trauma into rhetorically driven accounts of carnage and agony. They addressed their writings to a national audience in hopes of obtaining legal redress and financial compensation from the federal government. Edward Partridge wrote an account that became the first three installments of "A History of the Persecution, of the Church of Jesus Christ, of Latter Day Saints in Missouri" that appeared in the *Times and Seasons* (the newspaper the Church began to publish in Nauvoo) beginning in December 1839. In that same issue of the *Times and Seasons*, Eliza Snow encouraged women to think of the widows who had lost their loved ones at Hawn's Mill and see how those women did not lose hope or faith, though she acknowledged the sorrow she felt when remembering that emblematic event of the Missouri persecutions.[19]

Still another history, titled *Expulsion of the Mormons*, was written by

John P. Greene, who then went on a tour of the eastern cities to raise awareness and inform citizens of the horrors of the Saints' Missouri experience. At a public meeting in Cincinnati on June 17, 1839, Greene recounted the murderous attack at Hawn's Mill and emphasized the killing of young boys, the suffering of women, and the plundering done by the militia. The *New York Spectator*, having reprinted a report from a Cincinnati newspaper, called Greene's narrative "indeed a tale of woe and suffering at which the heart sickens."[20] On September 16, 1839, Greene was in New York City, where he gave a speech to a large crowd at the National Hall. According to the *New York Morning Herald*'s coverage, Greene provided the horrifying details of the militia's massacre of Latter-day Saints "who were peaceably encamped on Shoal Creek, near Far West. This tragedy was conducted in the most brutal and savage manner." Greene described the terrible and gruesome condition of Church members during the militia's occupation in the massacre's aftermath, but the paper would not comment any further except to say that the "scene that presented itself after the massacre, to the widows and orphans of the killed, is beyond description."[21]

Parley P. Pratt later wrote that through such histories and appeals, the Saints "fondly hope that the coming generation in those two states will go to school and learn that the laws and constitutions of the United States do not result, when properly administered, in murder, plunder, robbery, house-burning, rape, and exile."[22]

By the fall of 1839, Joseph Smith was out of jail and ready to take the case of his people to the US federal government. With more than five hundred sworn affidavits made in Adams County earlier that year (including the one that named Vienna Jaques) and a petition to Congress describing the Saints' sufferings, he left for Washington, DC, with Elias Higbee and Sidney Rigdon on October 29, 1839.

Though Rigdon became ill along the way and briefly returned to Illinois, the Prophet and Higbee continued on, arriving in Washington on November 28, 1839. U.S. President Martin Van Buren met with the men the next day. Smith and Higbee presented the president several documents, including petitions and a letter from James Adams from Springfield, Illinois. Adams, in introducing why the men were in the nation's capital, wrote, "Their business is to seek redress for the recent outrages committed on them and their property in Missouri. Those outrages are unparalleled in the annals of civilized communities."[23] After browsing through a few of the documents presented, Van Buren told Smith and Higbee that the federal government had no jurisdiction, no authority, and could provide no justice or redress because the persecution in Missouri was a state matter. The meeting ended abruptly, with not a single word of support or encouragement from the nation's highest executive.[24] The Saints' first effort for redress from the federal government was thwarted.

While in the nation's capital, Joseph Smith and Elias Higbee also sought to make their case to Congress. Their written plea to the nation's legislative body is especially poignant because it contrasted the Saints' experiences, losses, and efforts for redress with the constitutional guarantees of life, liberty, property, and religious freedom. These fundamental American rights had been taken from them in Missouri:

> The Mormons numbering fifteen thousand souls have been driven from their homes in Missouri; property to the value of two millions of dollars has been taken from them or destroyed; some of their brethren have been murdered; some wounded and others beaten with stripes; the chastity of their wives and daughters inhumanly violated; all driven forth as wanderers, and many, very many, broken hearts and pennyless. The loss of property they do not so much deplore, as the mental and bodily sufferings to

which they have been subjected; and thus far without redress. They are human beings, possessed of human feelings, and human sympathies. Their agony of soul for their suffering women and children was the bitterest drop in the cup of their sorrows. For these wrongs and sufferings, the Mormons, as American citizens, ask; *is there no redress?* Yet, of all these rights and immunities, the Mormons have been deprived. They have, without a just cause; without the form of trial; been deprived of life, liberty and property. They have been driven from the State of Missouri at the point of the bayonet and treated worse than a foreign enemy; they have been beaten with stripes as slaves; and threatened with destruction if they should ever venture to return; Those, who should have protected them, have become their most relentless persecutors; and what are the Mormons to do? It is the theory of our Constitution and laws, that, for the violation of every legal right, there is provided a legal remedy. For ourselves we see no redress, unless it be awarded by the Congress of the United States.[25]

Unfortunately, Congress would not allow the Latter-day Saint men the opportunity to verbally present their petition. Instead, the Senate referred the whole matter to its Judiciary Committee, which examined the written petition but took no action. Instead, the committee gave its opinion that "the case presented for their investigation is not such a one as will justify or authorize any interposition by this Government."[26] Not even the disturbing account of the Hawn's Mill massacre could entice the committee to sympathize with the mistreated Saints. Like the president, the Senate committee indicated that the federal government did not have authority over the matter. Thus, Joseph Smith and his companion were left to return to Illinois empty handed and frustrated.

Despite these efforts, neither Vienna Jaques and Daniel Shearer nor any other Latter-day Saints received compensation from the federal government for their Missouri losses. Just as the efforts for redress and restitution failed, so did the marriage between Vienna and Daniel; the circumstances of the separation are not known.[27] No children came from their union. Vienna would not marry again.

CHAPTER 9

A Witness

Even as Joseph Smith and other Latter-day Saints pled their case to anyone who would listen in Washington, DC, Church members in Nauvoo embarked on establishing yet another settlement, a new gathering place, a new Zion. Smith now taught that Zion was anywhere the Saints gathered and that it would eventually encompass all of North and South America.[1]

Many Saints worked tirelessly to drain the swampy flat lands along the banks of the Mississippi River. Death was common as mosquitos carrying malaria bit the new settlers.[2] Many were affected by the disease in the summer of 1840. Vienna Jaques would again have an opportunity to use her nursing skills to aid the sick, though we do not have specific accounts of her work and service. Vienna's life in the Church's new gathering place in Illinois is sparsely documented, but she, like the other Saints, struggled mightily to build the Zion of their faith.

As summer turned to fall in 1840, a notable series of events took place. An ordinance was introduced that would shape Vienna's life and become a signature of the Latter-day Saint faith. In September 1840, she witnessed the first recorded baptism for the dead.

Joseph Smith had given a funeral sermon for Seymour Brunson on August 15, 1840, in which he publicly addressed the doctrine and ordinance of baptism for the dead for the first time, a feature of the then-developing concept of salvation for the dead.[3]

Seymour Brunson was a veteran of the War of 1812, joined the Church in January 1831, and had served proselytizing missions for the Church in Ohio, Kentucky, and Virginia before gathering with the Saints in Caldwell County, Missouri and ultimately Nauvoo, Illinois. He had served on the Nauvoo High Council.[4] Brunson passed away on August 10, 1840. The cause of Brunson's death was not revealed, but of his life and faith his obituary stated: "He has always been a lively stone in the building of God: he was much respected by his friends and acquaintances; he died in the triumphs of faith, and in his dying moments he bore testimony to the gospel he had embraced by which 'life and immortality was bro't to light.'"[5]

At the funeral services for Brunson, the Prophet Joseph Smith began by first emphasizing the power of Christ to transcend death. Brunson had been baptized and confirmed a member of The Church of Jesus Christ of Latter-day Saints and lived faithfully until his death. His salvation through Christ's atoning power and grace felt certain. But what about individuals who had not heard of Christ's restored gospel and had not had the opportunity to be baptized and live His commandments and ordinances faithfully? This may have been a question on many of the Saints' minds, but it was particularly poignant for a woman in the congregation that day. Her name was Jane Harper Neyman.

Jane grew up in Westmoreland City in western Pennsylvania.[6] She met and married a man named William Livingston Neyman in 1812 in Butler, Pennsylvania, a town about thirty-five miles north of Pittsburgh.

Three years later, Jane gave birth to a son named Cyrus in the town of Butler on June 14, 1815. Jane and William had a dozen children, nine of whom lived beyond childhood or infancy. How Jane and her family became acquainted with the Latter-day Saints is not known. However, she was baptized in 1838 and she and her family had moved to Nauvoo by 1840.[7] Cyrus had already passed away, though the circumstances surrounding his death are not known. Jane's firstborn son had died before he could hear the restored gospel of Jesus Christ.

During Joseph Smith's funeral sermon for Seymour Brunson on August 15, 1840, Smith began to read extensively from 1 Corinthians 15. Drawing from Paul's letter to the Corinthians, the Prophet reminded the Saints that "a man must be born of the water and of the spirit."[8] Joseph "then noted a particular widow in the congregation whose son had died without baptism." Next, he declared that Church members "could now act for their friends who had departed this life." He further emphasized that "the plan of salvation was calculated to save all who were willing to obey the requirements of the law of God." The Prophet of God had publicly declared the doctrine of vicarious baptism. Proxy baptism for deceased persons offered hope and comfort that loved ones who had passed could still obtain eternal life and exaltation. This brought to many of the Saints, including Jane Neyman, "glad tidings of great joy."[9]

Jane Neyman was a woman of faith who persevered through immense suffering. She had already lost her son Cyrus and, within a few weeks of Joseph Smith's momentous discourse, her husband, William, died on September 2, 1840. Death seemed ubiquitous that summer. The opportunity to perform saving ordinance work for the deceased brought hope. Vilate Kimball wrote a letter to her husband Heber, who was then serving a mission with the Twelve Apostles in England, stating, "The day was joyful because of the light and glory that Joseph set forth. I can truly say my soul was lifted up."[10] Jane mourned her husband's death with the comfort that he had been baptized and had embraced the Latter-day Saint faith while on the earth. She believed he would obtain eternal life. But she still worried about her son Cyrus, who had passed before their family was acquainted with Christ's restored gospel.

After her husband's death, Jane Neyman contemplated more deeply what she had heard from Joseph Smith on baptism for the dead a month earlier. Convinced by her prayerful seeking and the words of the Prophet, Jane believed she could serve as proxy for her son in the baptismal ordinance. Neyman went to Harvey Olmstead, a Latter-day Saint elder and friend, and asked him to baptize her for her deceased son Cyrus Livingston Neyman in the Mississippi River. The two soon headed to the river to perform the ritual. This happened on September 12, 1840. It was an incredibly significant moment in the history of the restoration.

On that occasion, Vienna Jaques, curious about this vicarious work and the salvation of her own ancestors, apparently got word that Jane was going to the river to be baptized for her son. How she came to find out is not known. But Vienna was deeply interested in the eternal salvation of her ancestors. She mounted a horse and rode the animal to the river.[11]

As Harvey Olmstead and Jane Neyman walked together into the river, Vienna urged her horse off the bank and into the water. Vienna and her steed inched closer. Harvey grasped Jane, the grieving widow and mother, by her right wrist and raised his right arm to the square and said aloud a baptismal prayer. There was no set prayer, no precedence for this event. Vienna listened to the ceremonial prayer and observed the ordinance as Harvey then dipped Jane into the river, submerging her under the cloudy water. The faithful Jane Neyman emerged feeling that she had been reborn, baptized for her son in the open waters of the Mississippi River. Vienna Jaques was a witness as the ritual practice of vicarious baptisms was born.

That evening, Joseph Smith learned that this baptismal ceremony had taken place. He enquired about the "form of words" Harvey Olmstead used for the baptism. Upon hearing the report from Olmstead, Smith approved the ceremony and stated that "it was proved that father Olmstead had it right."[12] Vienna Jaques, the witness, was also consulted. Vienna confirmed to the Prophet what she had observed and heard, reassuring him that it was done as described. She later testified that the words Olmstead used during that first vicarious baptismal prayer were "preceisely the same as was afterward used by the Elders."[13]

A few weeks later at an October 1840 general conference of the Church, Smith taught the doctrine again, this time in a more official capacity by explaining to the Saints the opportunity they had to "liberate their friends from bondage" and introduce to their dead ancestors the fullness of the gospel thereby giving them "the privilege of comeing forth in the first resurrection."[14] He gave more prescriptive instructions for the ritual of proxy baptisms. Phebe Carter Woodruff was present at the October conference and wrote to her husband Wilford, then proselytizing for the Church in England, that when someone was baptized on behalf of the deceased, the deceased would be "released from prison" and have the opportunity to be brought "into the celestial kingdom."[15]

The sermon from Smith "was listened to with considerable interest."[16] From this discourse, Latter-day Saint Vilate Murray Kimball understood that the faithful could be "baptised for all their kinsfolks that have died before this Gospel came forth." From the moment he first heard about Jane Neyman, the first baptism for the dead, and the reports from Harvey Olmstead and Vienna Jaques, Joseph Smith was anxious to make sure that the work was done in proper order. As Vilate Kimball informed her husband, "There is a particular order that the Elders have to administer in, and to presurve this order."[17] The teachings and efforts to regulate this ritual practice came from the Prophet, but it was the actions of ordinary Saints seeking to live their religion and to bless their deceased kin that brought it to life. The actions of women and men laboring together in the work of salvation informed the ritual practice of this new, expansive ordinance.

Smith's discourse led to an immediate implementation of vicarious baptismal ordinances among the Saints. Of this surge in baptismal activity, Vilate Kimball noted, "the waters have been continually troubled. . . . [T]here were sometimes from eight to ten Elders in the [Mississippi] river at a time baptiseing."[18] That fervor remained high among the Saints in Nauvoo; in a letter she wrote, Vienna later stated that she "was baptized in the river in Nauvoo for maney."[19] Indeed, Vienna Jaques acted as proxy for more than fifty baptisms for the dead while she lived in Nauvoo, a number larger than many of her contemporaries. She was baptized for friends and family, both male and female, including her father, Henry, her maternal great-grandmother, Elizabeth Cogswell, and her seven times great-grandfather, the English Protestant Martyr John Rogers.[20] Vienna became captivated by the doctrine and practice of ritual work for the deceased. She dedicated time for the rest of her life to this critical aspect of gathering Zion.

News about the ordinance work for the dead spread quickly. In December 1840, Joseph Smith wrote to the Twelve Apostles in England. He informed them, "The saints have the priviledge of being baptized for those of their relatives who are dead, who they feel to believe would have embraced the gospel if they had been privilidged with hearing it, and who have received the gospel in the spirit through the instrumentality of those who may have ben commissioned to preach to them while in prison. Without enlarging on the subject you will undoubtedly see its consistency, and reasonableness, and presents the gospel of Christ in probably a more enlarged scale than some have received it." But as to the performance of ordinance work for the dead, the Prophet stated, "this right is more particularly confined" to the temple.[21]

The practice of baptism for the dead made national news in the summer of 1841. Latter-day Saints had performed a vicarious baptism for the nation's first president, George Washington, and for its most recently deceased president, William Henry Harrison, who died on April 4, 1841.[22] Word of those baptisms reached newspaper editors as far east as New York City. Several newspapers throughout the country contained columns explaining the ritual practice. The *Ohio Observer*, for example, informed its readership that Latter-day Saints taught that those who died "will have a second probation after death, and have the gospel preached to them. . . . Many of the spirits in prison do repent and believe, but being disembodied they cannot literally comply with the command of our Savior to be baptized. Hence if they have living friends in the body, the duty of these friends is to come and be baptized in their stead." The *Observer* continued, "Neither is this an idle speculation or dead faith among them. Many have actually been baptized for their deceased friends."[23] More than six thousand such baptisms occurred in the Mississippi River in 1841 alone.[24]

What started with two women, Jane Neyman and Vienna Jaques, and one man, Harvey Olmstead, in the Mississippi River on September 12, 1840, had already grown to thousands by the following year. Joseph Smith later taught, "The greatest responsibility in this world that God has laid upon us, is to seek after our dead."[25] In the next 150 years, the ordinance work for deceased individuals would explode to temples all over the world and for the eternal potential of hundreds of millions of people. Vienna was an early champion of proxy ordinance work having understood the principle, as taught in revelation, that work for the dead "cannot be lightly passed over" and that "their salvation is necessary and essential to our salvation."[26]

CHAPTER 10

The Temple

On January 19, 1841, Joseph Smith dictated a revelation in Nauvoo. Among its many tenets, the revelation declared the temple was the proper place to conduct baptisms for the dead. Hundreds of Saints, including Vienna Jaques, frequently entered the Mississippi River to be baptized on behalf of their deceased friends, family, and ancestors. "How shall your washings be acceptable unto me," the Lord stated, "except, ye perform them in a house which you have built to my name?"[1] The January revelation explained that members could continue to be baptized in the river only until the completion of the temple, where such baptisms would then be performed: "for a baptismal font there is not upon the earth; that they, my saints may be baptized for those who are dead, for this ordinance belongeth to my house."[2]

After a year of these baptisms, the Prophet told the Saints gathered in Nauvoo at the October 1841 general conference, "There shall be no more baptisms for the dead, until the ordinance can be attended to in the font of the Lord's House."[3] By the end of November, the Saints, so desirous to continue this sacred work, had completed a baptismal font "supported by

THE TEMPLE

twelve golden oxen," in the temple's basement. Though the whole structure was far from finished, the temple's font was dedicated, and the Saints immediately resumed baptisms for the dead in their proper place.[4] Once the font was dedicated, Vienna frequented it, anxiously engaged in the proxy work for her ancestors. She was baptized for dozens of her deceased relatives during the next year.[5]

Just as they had dedicated themselves to the work to construct the font, the Saints labored diligently to construct the entirety of the sacred edifice. Nauvoo was to be a temple city, a new expression of the City of Zion. It was to become a place where people from all over the world would come to learn about the gospel. Joseph encouraged Church members to "bring every thing you can bring and build a Temple unto the Lord a house into the mighty God." He obligated himself "to build as great a temple as ever Solomon did if the church will back me up."[6] As the Prophet spoke of the necessity of building the House of the Lord, the Saints responded by making it their highest priority.[7] Building a "Temple for the worship of our God" required the Saints to devote every tenth day, at least, to its construction. The Saints in Nauvoo labored together, unified toward this end.[8]

While the temple occupied substantial attention and resources, the vicissitudes of daily life continued in the burgeoning city on the Mississippi. Available records offer little insight into Vienna Jaques's life during the Nauvoo period. In addition to the work she contributed to the temple and the time she spent immersed in the practice of her faith, Vienna likely continued industriously in the variety of occupations she had long engaged: nurse, laundress, and care worker.

Vienna certainly continued to practice midwifery. She is obliquely referenced in a March 2–3, 1843, medical malpractice suit that Joseph Smith presided over in the Nauvoo mayor's court.[9] Charles Dana had charged Dr. William Brink with "causing premature childbirth by misdiagnosis and unjustifiable practices," which left Dana's wife, Margaret, in pain and poor health.

Dr. Brink was called to the Dana home on October 22, 1842. Margaret was distressed by fever and diarrhea. She was late in her pregnancy but was not in considerable pain when Brink arrived. The doctor gave her a "few powders," namely a cayenne pepper enema, incorrectly thinking that Margaret had miscarried. The enema was considered "unusual under the circumstances," according to witnesses who testified in the later trial. Following the procedure, Margaret began to experience excruciating pain.

Dr. Brink was called away in the night and he left the ailing woman. One of Margaret's friends, there in support, suggested to Dr. Brink that he ought to call someone with experience in childbirth to assist in the birth if he could not return in time. Brink noted that Margaret appeared to be weak and "bearing down." It was "proposed to call vienna," an apparent reference to the experienced midwife Vienna Jaques. Margaret was in distress when Brink left her to deal with another individual stricken with fever. Vienna likely attended to Margaret that night, but it is not known for certain how long she remained by Margaret's side. Margaret Dana remained in a distressed state until she delivered a healthy baby with the assistance of another midwife, Patty Bartlett Sessions, on October 24, some forty or more hours after Brink's unusual treatment.

Because of Brink's treatment, Margaret continued to experience constant back pain and incontinence. Though she did ultimately recover from this trial, Margaret died from cholera in Nebraska on the overland trail to Utah in 1850.[10] Brink was charged with "failing to perform correctly as [a] physician" in the treatment of Margaret. The case went on for two consecutive days. Though she was named in the court proceedings, Vienna Jaques was not called to testify in the case. Many others did testify,

THE TEMPLE

Nauvoo on the Mississippi River. This drawing, made looking east across the river likely from Montrose, Iowa, shows the relative size of the then-thriving city of Nauvoo. The unfinished Nauvoo Temple is prominently situated on the bluff overlooking the river while many residences and other buildings surround it on the peninsula.

and the female witnesses all seemed dissatisfied with Brink's treatment. The court ultimately found Brink at fault in the case. Joseph Smith ruled that Brink should pay Charles Dana ninety-nine dollars in damages and the totality of the court costs.[11]

In addition to developments in legal and civic administration, Nauvoo underwent momentous change in the early 1840s. As a resident of Nauvoo, Vienna would have observed the growing population as more and more Latter-day Saints gathered to the river city. The purpose of the gathering, Wilford Woodruff explained, was "to build unto the Lord an house to prepare them for the ordinances & endowments washings & anointings &c. . . . If a man gets the fulness of God he has to get in the same way that Jesus Christ obtained it & that was by keeping all the ordinances of the house of the Lord."[12] Since revelation designated Nauvoo as a temple city and explained why that was essential, the Saints had looked forward to additional priesthood blessings and authority in connection with the temple. A temple must be built, the revelation declared, because "there is not a place found on earth that [the Lord] may come to and restore again that which was lost unto you, or which he hath taken away, even the fulness of the priesthood."[13]

Joseph Smith first initiated new temple-related ordinances on May 4, 1842, with a small group of men. Brigham Young and fellow apostles Heber C. Kimball and Willard Richards were among those who received an "endowment" on that date, along with "certain instructions concerning the priesthood."[14] On May 26, 1843, he reassembled the same group (only two were missing) and repeated the earlier ceremony and instruction. This served to prepare them for being sealed to their wives and for additional temple-related teachings. Several couples, including Brigham Young and Mary Ann Angell Young, were sealed together for eternity a few days later.[15]

Vienna and the Saints listened as Joseph Smith taught them more about their eternal potential and celestial glory. In April 1843, for example, the Prophet explained that "the same sociality which exists amongst us here will exist among us" in the life to come. The nature of society in heaven, then, would maintain the earthly, familial ties in the next life. That sociality would be sealed in the eternities through rituals and ordinances performed on the earth through priesthood authority.[16]

An editorial in the Church's newspaper spoke of the importance of sealing. "Besides repentance, baptism, reception of the Holy Ghost, and many other essentials," the *Times and Seasons* article declared, "UNION of male and female, both temporal and spiritual, is of as much importance before God as all the rest; for the man is not without the woman, neither is the woman without the man in the Lord. And again, what God hath joined together, let not man put asunder, for the especial reason, that all contracts for time and eternity, have to be made while we sojourn in the flesh: 'In the resurrection they neither marry, nor are given in marriage, but the great lineage, through the priesthood, and the everlasting Covenant sealed on earth, and sealed in heaven, continues throughout all generations.'"[17]

As spring progressed into summer in 1843, Vienna and the Saints listened with interest as Joseph unfolded more doctrine on ordinance work such as sealings, including those by proxy to deceased spouses. Latter-day Saint Jacob Scott disclosed how a vicarious sealing would be enacted. If a man "desires to be married to his deceased wife," Scott told a family member, "a Sister in the Church stands as Proxy or as a representative of the deceased in attending to the marriage ceremony."[18]

Sealings also appeared to unite members of the Church into one family, a sociality that they believed would continue into the eternities, forming an eternal, unbroken chain amongst the faithful. Joseph Smith indicated that "he could not reveal the fulness of these things until the Temple is completed."[19] Nevertheless, a sealing to Joseph Smith, as Heber C. Kimball told his daughter Helen Mar Kimball, would ensure her exaltation and that of her family and kindred. Just as Vienna had been captivated by baptism for the dead, she became equally interested in the eternal possibilities offered by sealings. She had a desire to be sealed and have the sociality with the Saints continue into the next life, even though her relationship with her estranged husband Daniel Shearer did not entice her to seek a sealing with him. Her time for a sealing for herself would have to wait.

The gathering of Saints in Nauvoo grew the river city's population and influence. Work on the temple continued apace. The Saints received gospel messages and revelatory insights on doctrine and the work of salvation and exaltation. But, as they had experienced in their previous efforts to build a Zion community, ominous clouds of trouble soon rolled over them. Vienna Jaques knew these signs of turmoil all too well. She had experienced some of the most difficult moments in the faith's young history. What was on the horizon would leave another indelible imprint of pain and anguish etched into her memory.

On June 27, 1844, after months of escalating tension, Joseph Smith and his brother Hyrum Smith were killed by a barrage of bullets in Carthage Jail. News of the murders reached Nauvoo and its citizens swiftly. It dealt a damaging, grief-inducing blow to the Saints. Upon hearing the news, Latter-day Saint riverboat captain Dan Jones stated, "It is unlikely that there was so much sadness in any city in the world as there was reigning over Nauvoo at that time. . . . Oh, the sorrowful scene to be seen in Nauvoo that day. There has never been nor will there ever be anything like it; everyone sad along the streets, all the shops closed and every business forgotten."[21] Latter-day Saint Zina Huntington Jacobs similarly described the experience of those sorrowful days and her loneliness of heart. "Little did my heart ever think that mine eyes should witness this awful [scene]," Zina confided in her diary.[22] The shockwaves wrought by the martyrdom reverberated through the solemn community.

The next day, the bodies of the slaughtered Church leaders were taken to the Nauvoo Mansion, Joseph Smith's residence. In turn, "the thousands made their way forward, sad and desirous of having the last look at their dear brethren whose solemn counsels and heavenly teachings had been music to their ears, lighting their paths and bringing joy to their hearts on numerous occasions." Vienna was almost certainly among the moving throng, many with tears streaming down their faces as they looked upon

THE TEMPLE

the somber scene of the blood-soaked martyrs who died as witnesses of the work and gospel of Jesus Christ.[23]

In the eighteen months following Joseph Smith's death, Vienna Jaques, like the rest of the Saints in Nauvoo, knew that her days on the beautiful Mississippi River peninsula were numbered.[24] Pressure to vacate the community once again mounted in 1845. Opponents to the Church rose in fury. In addition to the outside opposition, Church members faced a succession crisis that splintered their community. Several individuals stepped forward to lead the Church, creating confusion among the Saints. Amid the contest to fill the leadership void left in the wake of Joseph's death, Vienna Jaques—along with the vast majority of Church members—chose to follow Brigham Young. She recognized that the priesthood keys and the authority to administer the ordinances that unlock the eternal potential offered in the temple rested with the Quorum of the Twelve Apostles, and that Brigham Young was the leader of that body.

Brigham Young was committed to finishing the temple. In the face of growing opposition and while planning the removal of the body of the Church to the Rocky Mountains, he led the Saints' efforts to complete the beautiful, sacred edifice on the bluff overlooking the Mississippi River. As important to him as any other preparatory effort in anticipation of their move west was giving the Saints the opportunity of receiving their temple ordinances and blessings.

The temple and administering the ordinances therein was the focal point of Brigham Young's life at this time. Young's journal entry of January 17, 1846, demonstrates his commitment to the Saints: "Such was the anxiety manifested by the Saints to receive the ordinances of Endowments . . . that I gave myself up entirely to the work of the Lord in the Temple almost night & Day I have spent not taking more than 4 hours upon an average out of 24 to sleep --- & but seldom ever allowing myself the time

& opportunity of going home once in a week."[25] During the following week, Young was "entirely confined to the Sealings & anointings of the Saints."[26] Young worked tirelessly in the temple, attending to the endowment and temple ordinances for the Saints during this time. He ensured that all worthy Latter-day Saints received their temple ordinance before the arduous journey west.

Brigham Young spent nearly every waking hour in January 1846 in the temple. The over five thousand rituals performed equipped the Saints, they believed, with the necessary heavenly endowments and spiritual power to withstand the precarious future that faced them as they prepared to leave Nauvoo. Vienna Jaques was among the Saints who went to the dedicated Nauvoo Temple. On January 22, 1846, she received her temple ordinance blessings, which were available only to those who participated in building the temple. That day she was "washed, anointed, and endowed" in the house of the Lord. She had been endowed with a spiritual power to face the coming adversity.[27]

Sarah Rich, a Latter-day Saint woman with whom Vienna would travel across the plains, expressed her feelings about having received temple blessings. Needing to take a leap into the dark to begin the arduous journey west from Nauvoo, Sarah wrote, "For if it had not been for the faith and knowledge that was bestowed upon us in the temple . . . it would seem like walking into the jaws of death." Sarah continued, "We had faith in our Heavenly Father, and we put our trust in Him, feeling that we were His chosen people and had embraced His gospel; and instead of sorrow we felt to rejoice that the day of our deliverance had come."[28] The temple had cemented the faith and provided an unwavering measure of strength for the Saints to travel to a place unknown.

Two weeks later, Vienna would drive her horse and wagon through the snow and the mud of Iowa, beginning the next stage of her grueling life's journey. She would be joined by thousands of other Latter-day Saints headed west. They would eventually gather at the base of the Rocky Mountains and renew their effort to build Zion.

Vienna would again be on her own to travel to a place unknown. She and her husband Daniel Shearer had apparently separated in Nauvoo. They did not receive their endowments in the Nauvoo Temple at the same time (Daniel received his on February 3, 1846, while Vienna had received hers earlier on January 22, 1846) nor is there a record of them being sealed together. They did not travel from Nauvoo to Winter Quarters together. Shearer was assigned to the Sixth Wagon Company, a different company from Jaques. That they were endowed at separate times and assigned different companies indicates that Jaques and Shearer were separated at least by early 1846.[29]

Despite the separation, Vienna, apparently strengthened by her worship in the temple, was prepared to move west. She and the majority of the Saints departed from Nauvoo in February 1846, leaving behind the community they had worked so hard to build. Seeing the temple, the house of the Lord, fade into the background, Vienna faced an unfamiliar path. She was on the move again. A new gathering place in which to build a new temple and a Zion community awaited.

CHAPTER 11

ONWARD TO THE ROCKY MOUNTAINS

The evacuation from Nauvoo began as Saints crossed the frozen Mississippi River, landing south of Montrose, Iowa. From there the refugees headed in a westerly direction until they reached the Des Moines River. That river served as a boundary line. On the west side lay the northeast corner of the state of Missouri. The Saints headed north along the river—deeper into Iowa—to avoid crossing into a state that still had an active extermination order for Latter-day Saints. The main body of some ten thousand Saints departed from Nauvoo along the same course as spring 1846 bloomed.

For these exiles, the trek across Iowa was full of toil, sacrifice, and death. It was a brutal strain for the emigrants who had left Nauvoo in a harried manner. They lacked knowledgeable guides and faced miserable weather that made the terrain difficult, if not impassable at times. It took the lead camp 131 days to cover three hundred miles. The Saints headed in a generally northwesterly direction, slogging through the mud and the muck until they reached the eastern bank of the Missouri River, near present-day Council Bluffs, Iowa.

As they passed near or through Iowa towns, Eliza R. Snow wrote that these members of The Church of Jesus Christ of Latter-day Saints were mocked and treated with levity rather than "sympathy for our houseless situation," a refrain now common to this people of faith.[1] These religious refugees were delayed through Iowa by inclement weather, lack of supplies, a call to raise a battalion of U.S. soldiers, and a variety of other factors. When by July 1846 they had only gone as far as the Council Bluffs region, Church leaders decided to establish temporary winter settlements in this area on both sides of the river.

Amid dense groves of oak trees along the river, the Saints built and employed ferries to cross the narrow, greenish-brown waters of the Missouri River. Historical records are silent on the life and activities of Vienna Jaques during this period. She apparently lived on the Nebraska side of the river and likely stayed at a camp in or near the main Winter Quarters in 1846–47. That main camp was one of approximately ninety Latter-day Saint communities that housed the thousands of Saints scattered through eastern Nebraska and southwestern Iowa.

As in past settlements and cities, religious worship and order were paramount in this diaspora of settlements. For example, at the main encampment of Winter Quarters, blocks were divided into twenty small lots each; the city was eventually divided into twenty-two wards with a bishop in each who was primarily responsible for conducting religious services for ward members and aiding the poor.

Women's experiences during this winter sojourn emerge as both triumphant and tragic. They contributed in countless, often untold, ways to home, community, economy, and camaraderie. Among other contributions, women sewed, knitted, made clothing, and led the way in ministering to, dancing with, and singing to their fellow religionists. Latter-day Saint sisters cared for families, friends, and neighbors in poverty, hunger, sickness, birth, and death. Women like Patty Sessions spent significant time and expended much energy tending to the sick; some even "anointed and laid hands and [said] a blessing" upon those who were ill.[2] Reading of these experiences is riveting, and the telling of them reveals the expanding roles and expectations of women in the faith community at this crucial time. The Winter Quarters experience was an important moment in the development of women's spiritual gifts as the community of Saints adjusted to new social and familial dynamics during this time of movement and transition.[3] Moreover, the Winter Quarters experience enabled women to strengthen already close female bonds, providing not just solace and hope to survive the winter but also opportunities to thrive as healers, comforters, and overall contributors to the Church and its members.

All Latter-day Saints at Winter Quarters lived under harsh conditions amid great stress and uncertainty. They struggled with the climate, lack of proper nutrition, prairie fires, and death, especially the loss of children. The specter of death was always close, whether from illness, accident, disease, the harsh weather conditions, or dietary insufficiencies.[4]

Nancy Reeder Walker Alexander had three daughters and was expecting a baby when her husband, Horace, left with the Mormon Battalion, an army troop established to aid the United States in the Mexican–American War. On January 1, 1847, it was cold when Nancy gave birth to her son, and she had only a few blankets to keep her and the baby warm and dry. After she contracted pneumonia, family members sent fifteen-year-old Catherine Huston to care for her. Nancy had Catherine bring her Horace's boots, which she clung to as she cried. She died on January 28; her baby died a month later.

Winter usually hits hard in the upper Great Plains region. Unrelenting, even gale force winds bring arctic blasts of cold and snow. To survive, people needed food and supplies. When the winter of 1846–47 set in, so did hunger. Though small game had been plentiful in the fall, by winter, Newel Knight noted, "our meals are often scanty."[5] In the face of these hardships, the Latter-day Saints relied ever more heavily on family, friends, and faith.

At Winter Quarters, the Saints proved their discipleship and determination to continue the Lord's work. An excerpt from a letter one Saint wrote from the temporary winter settlement on the Missouri River gives insight. "In the wilds of North America is the residence of your affectionate sister," Ursalia Hastings Hascall wrote. Hascall proclaimed that she was not "unhappy and suffering, no, far from it, nor none of our family," because, she declared, "there is nothing that would induce me to leave the company of the saints of God, unless it is the salvation of my friends and dear relatives."[6] These conditions help explain why spiritual practices were so important. As with so many of her fellow Saints, Ursalia's faith and her conviction that she was on the Lord's errand helped bring happiness during a time of immense trial. Vienna Jaques likely felt the same.

As the calendar year turned to 1847, Brigham Young seemed pleased with the efforts of the Saints. In a letter to Charles C. Rich on January 4, 1847, Young commented on the multiplication of righteous teachings and prayer meetings in Winter Quarters. "We have had quite a reformation at this place of late," the Church leader declared, along with "good feelings prevailing in the breasts of the Saints."[7] As Young rejoiced that the Saints were improving, his counsel for Church members to remain humble, patient, and work toward righteousness did not cease.

Amidst those teachings Brigham Young prepared for the next stage of the trek to the Rocky Mountains. He appointed various individuals to lead companies to go West. He organized the wagon company he would lead at a spot west of Winter Quarters on the Elkhorn River. The Vanguard Company, as it came to be known, began traveling to the Rocky

Mountains on April 16, 1847. Latter-day Saint Nathan Porter observed that this company departed eastern Nebraska "in se[a]rch of a place for the church to locate" and that Young had given "instructions for as many as could make the necessary outfit for them selves & families, to follow immediately on their track."[8] Young's company would arrive in the Salt Lake Valley more than three months later.

Vienna Jaques prepared herself, her animals, and her wagon for the trek to the Rocky Mountains. She was assigned to travel with the Charles C. Rich Company, which left the Elkhorn River area west of Winter Quarters, near present-day Omaha, Nebraska, on June 21, 1847. Just eleven days earlier, Vienna celebrated her sixtieth birthday. Now she prepared to drive her own wagon team across the plains.

While Vienna readied herself and her wagon to travel to the Rocky Mountains in June 1847, her estranged husband, Daniel Shearer, remained in the Winter Quarters area. He appears to have remained near the settlements surrounding the Missouri River for five more years. He finally departed from Pottawattamie County, Iowa, in June 1852 with the William Morgan Company.[9] Despite the difficulties with Daniel, Vienna seemed to always look forward and to find ways to contribute anew to building Zion. This time, looking ahead meant an arduous journey across the plains and through treacherous mountain passes.

Vienna was one of the 126 individuals in the Charles C. Rich Company when it began its journey from the outfitting post on the Elkhorn River, about twenty-seven miles west of Winter Quarters, Nebraska. The demographics of Rich's company were such that there were more women and children than men. Sarah Rich, one of the women in the company, remembered that they were "not verry Strong in number of men for there was more wimon and children than men in our camp. So we realised that we must be humble and prayrfull and put our trust in the

Lord and it was through his mercy and kind care that Saved the people on this daingerous jeorney for we praid to the Lord in faith and he answerd our prayrs for he will hear those that trust in him and obey his laws as given through his prophets."[10]

Many women, like Vienna, drove teams of cattle, oxen, or horses. Mary Ann Phelps Rich, another woman who, like Vienna, had no children, volunteered to drive a wagon team. Charles C. Rich was unsure if Mary Ann and another of his wives (plural marriage being practiced among the Latter-day Saints at that time, a custom that will be further discussed in coming chapters), Emeline Grover Rich, were capable of driving the team, but the women convinced him of their abilities. Mary Ann later said, "We persuaded him to try us one day and see. We did so well that we had our teams every day after that as regular as the men did until we arrived in the valley."[11] Jane McManagle Sherwood also traveled alone as her husband, Henry Sherwood, traveled in the Brigham Young Vanguard Company that had left months earlier.

The writings of other Rich Company travelers provide insight into what Vienna would have seen or experienced along the trail. Nathan Porter, one of the participants of Rich's Company, described the route they took. It followed the course of the North Platte River northwest across the Nebraska plains to Fort Laramie on the eastern edge of present-day Wyoming. "The trail led us a cross on to the Platt[e] River," Porter recalled. The company proceeded in two columns, "which was maintained for some five hundred miles."[12] As they journeyed up the Platte River, the company entered "Buffalo Country." They "saw maney large heards [herds] of buffalo" roaming the plains. At times the company suffered much from hunger, but not in buffalo country.[13] On July 17, 1847, Charles C. Rich wrote in his journal, "This morning we saw a large herd of buffaloe over the river on the south side, numbering several thousands;

after starting we saw several small herds in the bottom; we went after them. Got out into the bluffs about 3 or 4 miles and saw large herds; there seems to be no end to them. I should think there were ten thousand at least in sight in every direction. My company killed two large bulls that would weight 8 or 9 hundred lbs. each."[14]

On days when company members killed buffalo, they stopped for a camp and a feast.[15] The women would "wash iron and cook while the men folks repaird up there waggons and let there teames rest and recrute up."[16] At some camps, "the company would get together and we would have a dance in the evening on the grass."[17] "The days were not all filled with hard work," remembered one of the company's participants. "We sometimes went into camp for a few days' rest, and as there were musicians along, we often had a dance."[18] Occasionally, they would have visits from Native peoples, who came into camp to trade.[19] On Sundays, they would rest from their labors and meet to hear gospel messages.[20]

The company took a course more directly west from Fort Laramie, until they reached the Sweetwater River and, later, the South Pass, whereupon it began its southwesterly descent into the Salt Lake Valley.[21] Near Fort Bridger, the company received an unexpected visit. Brigham Young and several members of the vanguard company were returning east to Winter Quarters.

"We were overjoyed," Emeline Grover Rich reminisced as she described the meeting with Brigham Young on the trails. The members of the Charles C. Rich Company were worn out, having been three months on their journey. To hear from the Church leader "that they had found and located a stopping place for the Saints" brought inexpressible joy to the weary group of refugees.[22] Mary Ann Phelps Rich recalled, "President Young and his company stayed with us one day to talk and preach to the people, telling us what to do and how to do, and whatever we did to sustain the authorities that were placed over us, and we all felt well after that and felt as though we would do our duty as far as we could Brigham Young and his company resumed their journey eastward and we traveled on to the valley. The roads were terrible, the mountains bad, the teams weak and it was very cold, but we were not discouraged."[23] Young's visit gave the Rich Company the hope and assurance, though weak and tired, to muster the strength to complete the last one hundred miles of the trek to the Great Salt Lake.

Vienna Jaques and the members of the Charles C. Rich Company arrived in the Salt Lake Valley on October 2, 1847. In all, they traveled more than one thousand miles from the Elkhorn River to the Great Salt Lake Valley. They traveled as few as two miles and as many as twenty-three miles per day, excepting days for rest and Sundays.[24] Vienna was among the first fifteen companies to depart the Nebraska plains for the Great Basin in the first year of immigration and among the first 1,800 Latter-day Saints to arrive in Salt Lake City that year.[25]

CHAPTER 12

A LITTLE MILK

When members of The Church of Jesus Christ of Latter-day Saints entered the Salt Lake Valley in July 1847, their wagons held the meager belongings needed for them to survive in the Great Basin. In their flight past the western boundaries of the United States, they had trekked across the Great Plains to establish communities at the base of the Wasatch Mountains. These settlements soon became part of Utah Territory, the governmental precursor to the State of Utah. Having reached the end of one journey when they entered the Salt Lake Valley, they began a new journey to remake the landscape. The Saints relied on their religion and its strict organization and principles of community in order to survive and ultimately thrive. Community-minded cooperation would prove crucial to Latter-day Saint efforts to master a difficult terrain.

Like others who wintered in the valley, Vienna Jaques struggled to survive. She braved the freezing cold and snowy conditions, living in her wagon in the heart of the burgeoning Salt Lake City settlement. For more than a year, she laid down for rest each night in that wagon bed; many other individuals and families likewise slept in their wagons or makeshift tents. By October 1848, her wagon cover had become so tattered and rotted that it no longer offered protection. She could not stand it any longer. She needed a permanent place to call home.

Vienna procured some paper and jotted a letter to Brigham Young, the man who had been sustained as Church president on December 27, 1847. The faithful woman had long respected prophetic direction. She had left a well-to-do existence along with two properties in the eastern United States to gather with the Saints. She moved to Missouri following revelation and Joseph Smith's guidance back in 1833. She had been promised by revelation that she would be rewarded and that she would "receive an inheritance" in the land of Zion.[1] Her patience, as she faced another winter in a tattered wagon, apparently ran thin.

She asked President Young for a lot of land in Salt Lake City. He told her to "hold on." In her letter, she requested an answer to the question of how long she must wait for her land. Her houseless situation had troubled her for some time. She was especially troubled when William W. Phelps had told her that "there was no Lot for me any where within a great distance from where the Temple is to be." According to Vienna's letter, Phelps offered her "to come into his family," probably as a plural wife, and to build her a house. She stated simply, "I cannot accept the offer."[2] Though impoverished and without adequate housing, she was willing to place her trust and all material possessions in the hands of the Church president.

"Now if you think I am worthy to have a lot or part of a lot," Vienna pled, "let me know where to live so I can have my adobes hauled on to the same place." She had prepared and already obtained the building materials to construct her new abode. She said to Young, "I will endeavor to build as neat a house as others do, so as not to disgrace your city." She penned a simple, additional request: she wanted to have her place of residence located close enough "so that I can walk to the place of worship."[3] She was willing to persevere through her poverty, but she needed help and a parcel of land.

Having her own land would permit her to till, plant, and live from her efforts. Settlers faced many challenges in producing food. Late season frosts threatened vegetable and fruit growth. Infestations of pests left planters virtually helpless. Swarms of crickets began to threaten the Saints' crops in the summer of 1848. Harriet Young wrote, "to our utter astonishment the crickets came by the millions sweeping everything before them. They first attacked a patch of beans for us, and in twenty minutes there was not a vestige of them to be seen. They next swept over the peas, then came into our garden and took everything clean. We went out with a brush and undertook to drive them, but they were too strong for us."[4] Latter-day Saint settlers were rescued as large flocks of gulls devoured the crickets, allowing the settlers to salvage some of the harvest. The gulls—viewed by the Saints as heaven-sent—made an enormous difference between disaster and a respectable harvest in 1848. As the winter of 1848 progressed, many settlers satiated their hunger with rawhides, sego lily bulbs, thistles, wolf meat, and dead cattle. Latter-day Saint leaders initiated rationing among the settlers. Each person was allotted a half-pound of flour per day.[5]

While the timing and circumstances surrounding the acquisition of the land is unknown, Vienna obtained a parcel on Third East Street between First and Second South in Salt Lake City's Twelfth Ward by 1850.[6] A reminiscent account stated that Jaques lived "below" the Snelgrove family, who lived on Third East between South Temple and First South Street.[7] A later Sanborn map shows an adobe home with an outbuilding and an animal corral at 123 South Street, which corresponds with the description of her land on Lot 3, Block 50, Plat B in Salt Lake City.[8]

In order to allocate lands in a systematic and efficient manner, Church leaders had Salt Lake City surveyed. Brigham Young had directed Henry G. Sherwood, husband of Jane Sherwood, to survey the area just four days after the vanguard company arrived in the Salt Lake Valley. The product of the survey was a city plat of 114 ten-acre blocks, including a block for the construction of a temple. Sherwood drew the plat following the pattern of the City of Zion that Joseph Smith had established by revelation in 1833. The temple was to be the physical and spiritual center of the city, with streets radiating outward block by block in perfect order. The same day that he directed Sherwood's work, Young declared, "No man should buy any land . . . but every man should [have] his land measured off to him for city and farming purposes, what he could till. He might till it as he pleased, but he should be industrious and take care of it."[9] Much like the previous iteration of the law of consecration, Latter-day Saint men and women settlers were to be stewards of their property, not absolute owners; the Church leadership would be responsible for distributing the land. Beginning in 1848, lots were assigned to men who requested land; only a few single women received lots.[10] Vienna Jaques was one of those women.

Outside of the temple block, each city block was divided into eight lots, each one and a quarter acre in size. Lots were large enough to provide space for a house, a garden, domestic animals, feed and food storage, and fruit trees. With one house per lot, set back from the road some forty feet, the city began to have an open and consistent look throughout. Shortly after arriving in the valley, Church leaders divided Salt Lake City into wards, geographical ecclesiastical units headed by bishops. Vienna's lot was in the Salt Lake City Twelfth Ward, which was first presided over by Benjamin Covey, and, by 1856, by Leonard W. Hardy, a fellow Massachusettsan who was baptized by Orson Hyde during the proselytizing efforts that were greatly aided by Jaques in 1832.[11] The parcel of land Vienna would call home was close enough to walk to the temple.

At sixty-one years old, the energetic and still very capable Vienna went to work cultivating her Great Salt Lake City property.[12] Like other Latter-day Saint colonists, Vienna quickly built her shelter, likely with the help of laborers she paid. Individuals made use of unfired or adobe bricks for their homes as they were the most affordable and obtainable building material in the valley. Adobe bricks were created from the plentiful clay and sand dug from the area, especially from the banks of creeks along the Wasatch Mountains. Some log homes were built, but there were simply not enough accessible trees to make wood construction practical—especially because wood was so important for cooking and heating.[13] The adobe shelters were somewhat comfortable for the time and location, but as Eliza Marie Partridge Lyman wrote, "We are glad to get this much of a shelter but it is no shelter when it rains for dirt roof lets the water through and the dirt floor gets muddy which makes it any thing but pleasant." Vienna was likewise grateful for her home and lot of land. She lived alone in a "small adobe house"[14] that a neighbor described as a "pretty little house" that had "shutters and was quite up to date." She resided in this house for the rest of her life.[15]

After moving from Boston to Kirtland to Jackson County to Clay County to Caldwell County to Nauvoo to Winter Quarters and to Salt Lake City, Vienna had finally found the place to settle down in peace as she had been promised by revelation in 1833. She had endured many trials with patience, but now saw the promise of revelation as she went to work on her land of inheritance. An irrevocable gift, actual real property, a piece of land to make fruitful.

In addition to her efforts to cultivate her property, Vienna participated in various organized activities. She made her living as a nurse and remained connected to the healthcare community.[16] In 1852, for example, she attended meetings of the Female Council of Health. This council discussed medical matters "including distinctly female concerns," health issues, and remedies. The council also discussed the importance of taking care of spiritual health. Phoebe Angell, a midwife and the mother of Mary Ann Angell Young (Brigham Young's wife), presided over the council, which met twice monthly.[17] Vienna Jaques participated in this council and lent her decades-long practical wisdom to it. She, like other women, developed expertise in the systems of childbirth and attentive ministrations.

As a medical practitioner, Vienna was called in by other council members to consult on difficult cases.[18] A reminiscent account tells of Jaques's healthcare endeavors and skill. Claire Noall wrote that her "Aunt Louie was born, the first child to arrive in the 3rd East house. Several others followed, but no doctor attended their births. Vienna Jacques was the midwife for each. . . . A sister six years younger than Aunt Louie was stricken with typhoid. Mrs. Jacques helped the mother take the child through this sickness. They used to give her steam baths, by seating the little girl in a chair that either had no bottom or else a perforated one. In a kettle of hot water, placed under the chair there was some concoction of herbs which threw off an aromatic odor as the water steamed. When the water cooled, the women heated it by adding boiling water to it. The child lived, but she was rather sickly."[19] Vienna, like other female caregivers and midwives, was an essential part of the fabric of her community. She provided trained care during births and emotional and physical support to help mothers in need. In this case and likely in others, Vienna put her skill set to effective use to assist with childbirth and the unending tasks of domestic life, from cooking and cleaning to laundry to milking farm animals.

Vienna provided "essential services to bring the next generation into the world."[20] Just as she had given aid to the members of Zion's Camp and was called to assist or give advice in childbirth in Nauvoo, Vienna was often called upon to provide expert care to her Twelfth Ward family. She was among a community that provided consistent companionship and care to other women. This was a privilege that other western women were less likely to have because of their relative isolation in sparsely populated regions. They also lacked the community relationships and support that Latter-day Saint society provided.[21] Vienna frequently helped her neighbors with food preparation, childcare, chores, and the administration of remedies. She shared her time, talents, and wisdom freely in both the Female Council of Health and with the Saints in Salt Lake City.

Vienna even invited outsiders to attend the Female Council of Health meetings. Elizabeth Ferris, who came from New York with her husband Benjamin G. Ferris (he had accepted the appointment of secretary for Utah's territorial government), was in the Salt Lake Valley for about six months in 1852. During this time, Elizabeth became acquainted with Vienna, who frequently visited the boardinghouse where Elizabeth stayed in the city. Vienna invited her to attend a Council of Health meeting on April 5. In writings about her experience in Utah, Ferris labeled the council as "a sort of female society, *something like our Dorcas societies*, whose members have meetings to talk over their occasional various aches and pains, and the mode of cure."[22] Dorcas societies were named after a woman described in the biblical book of Acts, and they provided care and clothing for the poor—particularly widows. Ferris derided the Latter-day Saint Council of Health, writing that those who attended this "important assemblage," with a few exceptions, "belonged to the lowest class of ignorance."[23] Despite the kindness of Vienna Jaques, whom Elizabeth Ferris called her "guide-book," Ferris insulted the council and its members, calling them "stupid" and full of sensuality that "had swallowed up all pure womanly feelings" because many of them chose to participate in plural marriages.[24]

Though she roundly ridiculed Latter-day Saints and held a general prejudice against them as a people, Elizabeth Ferris wrote with some respect for Vienna. For example, Ferris stated that Vienna made some focused remarks in the health council meeting she attended.[25] Furthermore, in language similar to the early New England newspapers who described Vienna as an intelligent woman in 1831, Ferris surmised that Jaques would have been a "Women's Rights champion" had she remained in the eastern United States. Ferris described Vienna as "in every respect, a unique specimen of womanhood—tall, stout, bony, square-cornered—with cold, yet eager gray eyes."[26] "She has great industry, and struggled bravely through all the troubles" the Saints had faced, Ferris opined.[27]

At the same time, however, Ferris also derided Vienna, calling her, among other labels, "a curiosity." On January 24, 1852, she dedicated an entire day's worth of writing to Vienna. "If ever a menagerie of human beings should be gathered together by some enterprising Barnum, I now bespeak for her the post of lioness of the collection," Ferris wrote mockingly of Vienna. Despite the kindness and attention Vienna gave Elizabeth, the visitor repaid her with snide commentary and disparaging personal attacks. Though Elizabeth Ferris considered Vienna's spiritual views as "religious absurdities," she, like the New England newspapers had in 1831, praised Vienna's sensibilities, which displayed "Yankee shrewdness and thrift."

In her day-long journal entry on Vienna, Ferris further described her place of residence as one of "a few spots fit for cultivation" in an otherwise "wilderness of rocky sterility." Again, Ferris juxtaposed Vienna as somewhat acceptable while still considering the rest of her religious cohort utterly unacceptable. Elizabeth Ferris proceeded to call Vienna's house "her solitary lair," a "curiosity shop" that the "penny saving New Englander" had kept through all the turmoil of movement from Boston to "Missouri and Illinois, where buildings were ruthlessly torn down over the heads of the widow and the orphan" and finally to Salt Lake City. These items were treasures to Vienna, even if Elizabeth simply found them to be "a lot of odd traps."

Elizabeth completed her journal entry by describing a day in the life of Vienna Jaques. "She often walks over her acre, to be sure that she has gathered in her whole crop." Ferris, the New York visitor, continued: "An inveterate gleaner she is, but not quite realizing the sweet pictures our artists give us of Ruth and Tamar of old. I take great delight in watching her as she sallies forth at evening, on the plateau north of us, after her cow. I readily recognize her old yellow marten fur cape – her wide cap-border flapping in the wind, under a comical-looking hood – and her dress, some of her own handiwork in spinning and weaving, just wide enough and none to spare, around her gaunt form. This notable dress is Bloomer enough to display a serviceable pair of brogans. Thus attired, and looking for all the world like a picture of Grant Thorburn in petticoats, she strides along, armed with a stout stick, bidding defiance alike to the tawny digger and the grizzly bear."[28]

Much can be gleaned about both the perception of Vienna Jaques and the biases of the writer of this passage. Ferris made an economic and social commentary on Jaques's impoverished condition and plain clothing that barely covered her, fuller skirts and larger sleeves being the women's fashion of the day. From the same details about Vienna's clothing that Ferris held in disdain, we could also glean that Vienna clung to everything she could obtain and was a force to be reckoned with. Vienna was a favorite character of Elizabeth Ferris, who published her observations and opinions for the world to read shortly after returning home to Ithaca, New York.

While Ferris compiled her account of her experiences in Utah, Vienna began participating in other community-based, organized efforts. She was living on her own in the Twelfth Ward in 1854 when she joined that ward's Indian Relief Society. There were many ways that Latter-day Saints tried to exert influence on the region's indigenous peoples—particularly the Utes, Paiutes, and Shoshone—including the creation of Relief Societies "for the purpose of making clothing for Indian women and children" as a way to "civilize" them.

The Saints had moved to the homelands of these and other indigenous nations. As the Saints' population increased and they colonized more of the productive lands in the region, conflicts with indigenous peoples likewise increased. Indigenous peoples had less and less access to natural resources and more and more need for food, clothing, and other essentials. The Saints responded in a variety of ways, including with female-led benevolent societies. Brigham Young explicitly encouraged women to "form themselves into societies" and meet in their own wards to make clothing for indigenous peoples.

Women responded immediately. During 1854, some twenty-two "Indian" Relief Societies were organized in Salt Lake City and outlying settlements, as part of the Latter-day Saint faith's broader efforts to maintain positive relations between settlers and the local indigenous population. Women made, gathered, or donated food, clothing, bedding, and cash, "to the church's Indian relief effort."[29] This was just one women-led work in early Utah, and Vienna Jaques contributed to it.

Later that same year, Vienna visited the Church Historian's Office. On November 29, 1854, the weather in Salt Lake City "was fine almost like spring."[30] Vienna walked north from her home, just over a block to

South Temple Street. There she took a left and headed west for just over two large city blocks. She walked past the recently completed Beehive House, the home of Church President Brigham Young, into the Church offices.

What prompted her visit to the historian's office is not known. Perhaps she received an invitation from the office employees who were, during the fall of 1854, "looking up & amalgamating items" about Joseph Smith's history and life from the fall of 1840.[31] Whatever the reason, Vienna entered the Historian's Office that late November day with a purpose. George A. Smith was the Church Historian and Recorder at that time, though it is not known if that was the person with whom she met. Vienna was there to affirm and attest to the story her friend Jane Neyman contributed to the Church Historian's Office regarding the first baptism for the dead. Neyman was in the Church Historian's Office that day as well, describing when she heard Joseph's first comments on baptism for the dead at Nauvoo and how she enlisted an elder to administer the rite on behalf of her deceased son Cyrus. Vienna was present and witnessed that seminal event in the Mississippi River in September 1840. She confirmed Neyman's account with the workers at the Historian's Office that day, chronicling for posterity the events of that momentous occasion.

Though Jaques was independent and self-reliant, she occasionally had to be strategic and resourceful in her relationships with men in order to navigate early Utah society and economy. In the fall of 1855, with winter approaching, for example, she needed to trade her cow for another. Jaques needed "a little milk this winter," as her cow had gone dry some two months earlier. She had attempted to trade with "every man" that she knew, including her ecclesiastical leader, to no avail, so she sent a letter to Brigham Young, the Church president and territorial governor (having been appointed to that position by U.S. President Millard Fillmore in

Detail of Vienna Jaques letter to Brigham Young, September 11, 1855.

1850), asking for assistance. She explained her dilemma to Young, stating that she did not "know how to live without milk" because she did not use "tea nor coffee nor meat," noting her strict adherence to the Church's Word of Wisdom provision.[32] Jaques then made a sales pitch, noting that her cow was "a very great eater & a very large cow" and proposed that Young take the cow to make a trade for another that would provide her with the sustenance she required. Jaques sweetened the deal by stating that she would even pay Young to make the transaction for her.[33] The outcome of this transaction is not known, but based on a later letter from Jaques to Young, it is likely that Young assisted her.[34] This letter and others from Jaques reveal the difficulties that she faced as a single woman in the male and Church-dominated Utah economy and the necessity of appealing for the assistance of men, primarily her ecclesiastical leaders, in times of need.

The experience of Latter-day Saint women in the Salt Lake settlements was both archetypal and unique. Just as in other communities, women were critical to the operation of every household. Wives, mothers, sisters, daughters, and children confronted the same challenges and difficulties as the men. They performed all the duties of home, from making, washing, and ironing clothing to churning butter, milking cows, or harvesting crops. They also bore and raised children, often with the help of competent nurses and midwives. The communal nature of Latter-day Saint society provided safeguards to sustain women and families in need. The tithing and donation of money, food, goods, clothing, and other materials not only helped public works and immigration, but it also provided for women and families in need. Despite hardships, Latter-day Saint women spearheaded efforts to create dramatic, scientific, and literary societies and to build venues for theater, music, dancing, and other cultural activities.

Vienna Jaques contributed to the community in many ways. From her adobe abode she made textiles; raised and milked her own cows; made her own butter and grew a garden of various fruits and vegetables; read incessantly and wrote letters (almost none of which survived); and occasionally took in elderly men in need of hospice and other care.[35] Jaques's industriousness and self-reliance remained trademarks during those difficult first years in the Salt Lake Valley. She continued to work as a midwife and nurse, offering assistance to her neighbors during childbirth and sickness.[36] Jaques, the "square-built, angular Yankee," even produced a rag hearth rug that was so beautiful and magnificent that she won a prize at the second annual exhibition of the Deseret Agricultural and Manufacturing Society—the present-day equivalent of a state fair—held in Salt Lake City in early October 1857.[37] Her contributions and experiences during the first decade of Latter-day Saint settlement in the Salt Lake Valley were both unique and common. She did all she could from her new home to help build a Zion community.

CHAPTER 13

A Sealing

Vienna Jaques believed deeply in the power and value of ordinance work performed in the temple, both for herself and by proxy for the deceased. She participated in the work of vicarious baptisms for deceased relatives while in Nauvoo. She had received the ordinance of the endowment in the Nauvoo Temple before she departed for the West. Vienna had not, however, been sealed to her estranged husband Daniel Shearer while they were both in Nauvoo.

Whenever Elizabeth Ferris inquired about her husband, Vienna had demurred to discuss him or her marital situation. "It seems she has a husband wandering somewhere about the earth," the erstwhile friend wrote about Vienna. Ferris noted that Vienna had "abandoned him to his fate," but that "she manifests some reserve" when pressed for more details. "His existence and whereabout," Ferris stated, "are mysteries which my profane curiosity has not been permitted fully to penetrate."[1]

What Vienna did not disclose was that Daniel had married another wife. After Vienna relocated to the Salt Lake Valley, Daniel remained in the Midwest where he married his second wife, Mary Wilkie. He and

Mary had moved to the valley by fall 1852, eventually establishing a home in the Salt Lake City Thirteenth Ward.[2] Vienna had no desire to be sealed to Daniel in 1846 and she remained averse to be united with him in her present life or for eternity in the 1850s.

Vienna did, however, wish to have a companion in the next life. Joseph Smith had taught that a marriage performed under priesthood authority, or sealed by that authority, could extend into eternity, and secure one's exaltation.[3] She wanted to be sealed to a man whom she regarded with the highest esteem. She wanted to be sealed to a man who would unlock her eternal potential and enable her to experience the highest degree of celestial glory.

According to revelation, that sacred work of sealing was supposed to take place within the walls of the temple. But the Saints had left their temple in Nauvoo and progress on a new temple in Salt Lake City moved slowly. While work on the Salt Lake Temple moved forward in fits and starts, Brigham Young authorized the construction of a smaller building where the Saints could receive ordinances including the endowment and marriage sealings. This building, a two-story adobe structure, was constructed in 1854 and 1855 on the northwest corner of the temple block. It was called the Endowment House.

Records indicate that Vienna Jaques visited the Endowment House on March 28, 1858, and participated in a special religious ordinance. As a believer in the doctrine of eternal sealings that would bind her to a faithful individual and ensure her eternal salvation and exaltation, she was posthumously sealed to Joseph Smith that day.[4]

Like it was for many women, plural marriage was a "great stumbling block" for Vienna Jaques. She admitted as much to the sojourner Elizabeth Ferris, or at least Ferris said she did.[5] In 1848, Vienna had declined William W. Phelps's overture to join his family as a plural wife, preferring to forge her own path and build her own house. She likewise declined other men's offers.[6] It seems she had no interest in being a second, third, fourth, or fifth wife of anyone.

The practice of plural marriage complicated the lives of women, Latter-day Saint society, and outsiders' perceptions of the Saints. Joseph Smith introduced this religious teaching to his followers in Nauvoo, but its actual practice was largely kept secret. In 1852, that changed. Church leaders in Salt Lake City made a clear, public announcement that Latter-day Saints believed in and practiced the marriage of one man to multiple women.

Though most outsiders argued as much, the Saints vehemently denied that this marital system was an outlet for male lust. Rather, its theology transformed male sexual desires into spousal and parental responsibility, while providing more women with an opportunity to marry and become a mother. A plural marriage and the sexual union of men and women was a religious incentive to bring spirits to earth and to raise them up to inherit what Latter-day Saints believed was the kingdom of God. As the historian Laurel Thatcher Ulrich explains, Latter-day Saint "men received power from God to give lives to those who wished to receive them. A woman's role was to receive those lives, by conceiving, bearing, and rearing righteous children."[7]

One visitor to Utah, a photographer and artist named Solomon Nunes Carvalho who accompanied John C. Frémont's 1853–54 expedition from Missouri to San Francisco, reported a conversation he had with some polygamist women that summarized feelings about plural marriage in Latter-day Saint society. He wrote, "I had several spiritual conversation[s] with these ladies on the spiritual wife system, they submit to it because they implicitly believe it to be necessary to their salvation." Plural marriage, then, was viewed through the lens of eternal possibilities. It was also viewed through the lens of family and love. The women to whom Carvalho spoke argued, "Cannot a father love six children? Why can he not love six wives?" The visitor concluded "that during a sojourn of near three months in Salt Lake City, I never observed the slightest indications of improper conduct, or lightness among them—neither by conversation or otherwise. Their young ladies are modest, and unassuming, while their matrons are sedate and stately. Polygamy is by no means general, there are hundreds of Mormons who have only one wife."[8]

Vienna Jaques made a similar observation to Elizabeth Ferris. Ever the good missionary, Vienna taught Elizabeth about the Latter-day Saint faith and its practice of plural marriage. After explaining the challenges she had with the doctrine, Vienna said, "It is not compulsory," indicating that if Ferris and her husband were to convert to the church, her "husband need not take another wife."[9] Not to get the eager missionary's hopes too high, Elizabeth quickly noted that plural marriage "is a point very difficult for us to get over."[10] The practice of plural marriage was something that weighed heavily on Vienna's conscience, though, as Ferris described, she "managed to choke it down with a wry face," because of her belief in and trust of Joseph Smith as a prophet of God.[11]

Despite Vienna's difficulties with plural marriage, many writers have speculated that Jaques was a plural wife of Joseph Smith while he was still living. The documentary evidence for this assertion is weak, though three sources point to the possibility. This first is an unsigned affidavit in Joseph F. Smith's 1869 affidavit book that contains Vienna Jaques's name but lacks pertinent details about a marriage or sealing and was not signed by Jaques. Like this affidavit, some other sworn statements in Smith's book appear to have been prepared beforehand and were later left uncompleted and unsigned by the named individual. This offers a possibility that Joseph F. Smith and others thought Jaques was a plural wife, but that she was not.¹² A second source is a reminiscent statement from Nancy Alexander, a woman who claimed that "the Mormon Prophet robbed" her family, reporting a rumor she heard in Kirtland in 1836 that Joseph Smith had a revelation "to lie with Vienna Jaques, who lived in his family." Alexander's statement of this rumor does not appear credible and does not match the known history of Jaques, as she never appears to have lived with Smith's family.¹³

The last source is a thirdhand account written in 1943 by Claire Noall, in which she reports to Fawn Brodie a conversation she had with her aunt Louie Richards, the daughter-in-law of Willard Richards. Noall apparently asked Richards if Jaques was one of Smith's plural wives. According to Noall's letter, Richards responded to Noall's query by stating "with no uncertainty" that Jaques "was sealed to him," referring to Joseph Smith.¹⁴ The letter neither indicates whether Richards had confirmed this assertion with Jaques, nor does it give any other details about the supposed union, including whether Richards believed it happened while Joseph Smith was still alive. After receiving Noall's letter, Brodie replied. She wrote that she wanted a friend, Vesta Crawford, to "try to check to see if she could find out a bit more about Vienna Jacques, and she may be calling you to arrange an interview with your Aunt Louie. What I should particularly like to know is whether Vienna was sealed to him during his lifetime or posthumously." No other records found in Brodie's papers provide evidence for Jaques's possible marriage to Smith.¹⁵ Nevertheless, Fawn Brodie appears to have taken Noall's thirdhand statement to mean that a "marriage took place while the prophet was alive," which statement she made in her 1945 biography of Smith.¹⁶

Jaques was posthumously sealed to Smith, but never stated that she was a plural wife. According to an account given by Joseph Smith III, Jaques explicitly denied being married to Joseph Smith as "one wife or as a plural one."¹⁷ It appears that all that can be said with certainty is that Vienna Jaques was sealed to Joseph Smith, but only after his death in June 1844. She was one of several women who were sealed to the Prophet after his death. Though they had not earthly unions, they could be sealed by proxy in hopes of an eternal connection to Joseph Smith.¹⁸

CHAPTER 14

A LITTLE TROUBLE

Much had happened in Utah and for the Latter-day Saints during the 1850s. The Saints felt under siege again in 1857 as the president of the United States sent a substantial portion of the standing U.S. Army to put down a supposed Latter-day Saint rebellion in Utah Territory. With the army en route to the Rocky Mountains, Brigham Young put the territory under martial law, Church leaders sent a legion to the mountains to protect the Saints, and local Latter-day Saints attacked emigrants on their way to California in what became known as the Mountain Meadows Massacre. During a winter standoff that kept the U.S. Army out of the Salt Lake Valley, the Saints began a mass movement away from Salt Lake City in what was dubbed the "Move South," only to return in the summer of 1858 as the army arrived and established a military fort, Camp Floyd, about forty-five miles south of Salt Lake City on the west side of Utah Lake.[1]

Vienna Jaques's experiences and feelings during those and other momentous events of the late 1850s are not found in the historical record. She did, however, go again to the Church Historian's Office early in 1859 to make a correction to an account of a past historical event. On February 22, 1859, a "clear and fine" Tuesday afternoon, Vienna walked just over half a mile from her home to the Historian's Office.[2] She had recently read a portion of Joseph Smith's history as printed in the *Millennial Star*, a Church periodical published in England since 1840. In the September 25, 1852, issue was an account of the tarring and feathering of Bishop Edward Partridge. Vienna was present in Jackson County, Missouri, on that day in July 1833 and had witnessed the aftermath of that heinous act.

The *Millennial Star*'s history of Joseph Smith depicted the events that led to the eviction of the Saints from Jackson County. That account stated, "And when Bishop Partridge, who was without guile, and Elder Charles Allen, walked off, amid the horrid yells of an infuriated mob, coated like some un-named, unknown biped, and one of the sisters cried aloud, 'while you, who have done this wicked deed, must suffer the vengeance of God, they, having endured persecution, can *rejoice*, for henceforth for them, is laid up a crown, eternal in the heavens' – surely there was a time of awful reflection, that man, unrestrained, like the brute beast, may torment the body; but God, in return, will punish the soul."[3]

Why Vienna was reading that issue of the *Millennial Star* that had been published more than six years earlier is unknown. Nevertheless, its contents prompted her to call "at the Historians office" that February afternoon, where she stated that "the history of Joseph Smith was incorrect as published in the Mill. Star, Vol 14, page 486, where it gives an account of Bishop Partridge's being tarred and feathered." Vienna told the Historian's Office employee "that she is the sister referred to, as crying aloud" in the *Millennial Star* version.

She then relayed the circumstances from her perspective and recollection. The Historian's Office employee wrote her account as follows: "At the time Bishop Partridge was tarred and feathered at Independence, the printing office was torn down, and the revelations were thrown into the streets . . . she looked and saw a figure passing, but did not recognize the Bishop, and asked, Where? The man replied, that he had just passed behind a house; she took two or three steps and saw him going along, encircled in a bright light, surpassing the ~~light~~ <brightness> of the Sun; She exclaimed Glory to God!, for he will receive a crown of glory for tar and feathers. She did not make this exclamation to any person, as she was alone at the time."[4] Vienna understood the importance of getting the history accurate, clarifying that she did not in fact say the words the *Millennial Star* account had attributed to the sister who "cried aloud." She provided her perspective. Her voice corrected the record and was valued by the Historian's Office.

The Historian's Office held something very dear to Vienna's heart. At some point, she had deposited the September 1833 letter Joseph Smith had sent to her during the trials in Jackson County, Missouri. Vienna had probably taken the letter to the Historian's Office after Joseph was killed at Carthage Jail. In November 1845, while still in Nauvoo, Church Historian Willard Richards wrote an epistle to the Saints asking "all those who have letters, or documents of any kind in their possession, which in any way relate to the History of the Church of Jesus Christ of Latter Day Saints, . . . to leave them with the Historian."[5] Vienna apparently acquiesced to that request. Though surprising given how significant the letter was to Vienna, the obedient disciple dutifully donated the "word of comfort" Joseph had sent to her more than twelve years earlier. For Vienna, like other Latter-day Saints, "history was ongoing and participatory."[6] She, as much as anyone else, was a part of the Church's sacred past and she contributed to its preservation and accuracy.

Just a week and a half after Vienna Jaques visited the Historian's Office to set the record straight on the tarring and feathering of Edward

THE LORD SPOKE HER NAME

Salt Lake City looking east along South Temple Street. This is a view that Vienna Jaques would have enjoyed as she often walked South Temple Street. Two of Brigham Young's residences, the Lion House and the Beehive House, are prominently featured. The Historian's Office was located across the street from Young's residences.

Partridge, Brigham Young "sent over to the Historian['s] Office after the autograph of Joseph Smith."[7] For unknown reasons, Young wanted a sample of his predecessor's signature, perhaps for a keepsake.[8] The Church Historian's Office acquiesced to the President's request. A Historian's Office employee then "cut off" Joseph Smith's name from "a letter that Joseph wrote himself & sent to Vienna Jaques." Why the Church Historian's Office decided to desecrate Joseph's September 4, 1833, letter to Vienna Jaques, out of the numerous samples of the Prophet's signature they had in the archives, is unknown. But that is the letter from which they chose to furnish Brigham Young with a signature of the founding prophet of the restoration.[9]

Six months later, Vienna Jaques had occasion to write a letter to Brigham Young. It had nothing to do with Young's disfiguring of the letter

Joseph Smith had sent her. Jaques wrote requesting advice on a "little trouble" she was having with Jacob Workman, a forty-seven-year-old Latter-day Saint whom she had charitably employed to "hall some rock & sand & clay & Adobies & put up a little cow stable" on her property, thereby working off a debt he owed her. To Young, she gave her appreciation for, she said, "You have always been willing to read my papers, that I have sent you, & have always answered to there call, this encourages me at this time, to lay before you" the matter with Workman. According to her letter, Jaques gave Workman money to purchase the adobe bricks and limestone. Workman had not completed the construction when, on July 20, 1859, he presented Jaques with a bill of charges amounting to $93.30, which made Jaques "nearly sick," especially given that cash in Utah was scarce and daily wages were low. She had acted charitably with Workman in the past, allowing him to borrow some of her hard-won resources, including more than a thousand pounds of flour and some money during the previous five years. Jaques noted that some of the flour was given at a time when flour was incredibly scarce and selling for ten dollars per hundred pounds.

Believing she was being taken advantage of, Jaques took the bill and her complaint to various men, including Leonard W. Hardy, then bishop of the Salt Lake City Twelfth Ward.[10] Hardy thought that Workman overcharged Jaques for hauling and for materials, for which Jaques had already given him money. Jaques then confronted Workman with Hardy's assessment, to which Workman assertively stated that "he would have all he had charged or he would go to higher powers to get it." Bishop Hardy was not willing to help Jaques further, and no one else was willing to mediate or give the single sister advice on the situation.[11] So she wrote to President Young.

Noting that Workman still owed her a larger debt than the bill he charged, Vienna felt "greatly imposed upon by Mr Workman." She wrote to the Church President, "if <I have> done wrong in trespassing on your time, or the order of, I hope you will overlook it, I shall not be hurt in my feeling, if you take no notice of what I have told you." She sent along the full bill of charges so that she might hear from Young "if I ought to allow him it all."[12]

She had to wait nearly eight weeks for a reply. On November 7, 1859, Brigham Young acknowledged the slowness of his reply and stated that "one circumstance and another" had prevented him from replying sooner. Young told Jaques that he asked Briant Stringham and Bishop Hardy to examine the bill and the work Jacob Workman had done on Vienna's property. Following their inspection, Young had Stringham, Hardy, and Workman to his office for a report. Stringham and Hardy informed Young and Workman that they thought Workman overcharged by $3.30 and that $90 even "would be right in the case." Workman said, "he did not want any more than was right," replying that he would take an additional five dollars off. He claimed that he did more work on the property than was represented in the bill and that $85 would suffice for his work.[13] Young did not acknowledge the fact that Vienna claimed that Workman owed her more than the original charge, but concluded by writing, "From all I can learn, I should presume that the bill is now quite reasonable, and trust it will prove satisfactory to you."[14] Young closed his letter, "Your Brother in the Gospel." This negotiation would have taken about 9 percent off the bill. It is hard to imagine that Vienna found this resolution, to which she was able to give no input beyond lodging the complaint in the first place, satisfactory. There is no evidence of any further correspondence or a response from her, but it is assumed that Vienna paid Workman to settle the matter before the year closed.

The 1860s saw even more momentous events. The United States

experienced a brutal Civil War, which brought an end to the institution of slavery. Utah saw the departure of the U.S. Army from Camp Floyd and the arrival of a new contingent that established Fort Douglas on the mountain bench overlooking Salt Lake City. Following the war, the nation focused its attention westward, seeking to unite the fractured country. The construction of a transcontinental railroad promised to bind the nation together. As railroad companies employed workers to furiously build the iron road, the route came through and united at Promontory Point in Utah. In May 1869, the nation celebrated the completion of the transcontinental railroad. Traversing the trans-Missouri West had taken months for Vienna Jaques and other pioneers. That same route could now be crossed in just days. Transportation had been revolutionized.

Again, during this transformative decade, we only see glimpses of the life of Vienna Jaques. One such event was the second annual Zion's Camp reunion. Vienna was not a member of the Zion's Camp company, but she had been in Missouri when the expedition arrived. She provided essential healthcare to and succor for the camp participants. Her contributions had long been recognized by Church leaders.

On Tuesday afternoon, October 10, 1865, a "wet and cloudy" day, Brigham Young called the meeting together at Salt Lake City's Social Hall.[15] After an impromptu choir led by Young sang "Hark, Listen to the Trumpeters," Joseph Young made "a few remarks recounting the scenes of hardship endured in the arduous journey of Zion's camp."[16] Three long tables were filled with food for a sumptuous dinner. Following dinner was dancing, more reminiscences, and remarks and singing from various individuals. At 10:15 p.m., supper (a light meal served late in the evening) was announced. The same trio of activities—speaking, singing, and dancing—continued until nearly three in the morning of October 11. Vienna attended as a guest of Brigham Young and his wives, Mary Ann and Emeline Free, at this event.[17] She was one of approximately one hundred individuals in attendance that night.

Reunions such as the Zion's Camp event that Vienna attended helped to forge a "sense of place and a sense of belonging among members of these older generations," providing "a degree of self-validation for individuals." They spoke of and celebrated the history of their labors for the kingdom of God when it was in its infancy. Those commemorative events helped ensure that the achievements and experiences of aging generations were not forgotten. That their accomplishments were shared and celebrated established a foundation for a collective memory for the Church community.[18]

Nearly eighteen months passed from her attendance at the reunion before Vienna is found again in historical sources. She visited the Historian's Office again on April 2, 1867. On that date, she inscribed her autograph on the bottom border of a photograph of herself taken by Latter-day Saint photographer Edward Martin. Martin's shop was on the west side of East Temple (now State) Street between First and Second South, just a couple of blocks west of Vienna's home. She had likely visited Martin's to have her photograph taken that year as she was turning eighty years old. In the photo, Vienna is seated with her left elbow resting on a blanket-covered table, her weathered left hand clasped around her right. Her dress is plain. She wore a dark, long-sleeved, hand-sewn dress. She sported a bonnet neatly tied beneath her chin. Her stoic, reserved countenance is belied by piercing eyes fixated on the camera and photographer. Those penetrating eyes provided an opening to the stories she had to tell.

Vienna had likely given a copy of the photograph to the Historian's Office for a visual record of her. History was important to her. Her visual appearance now preserved, she added her name and handwriting to this fragment of her and the Latter-day Saint experience. On the reverse of the photograph, a Historian's Office employee inscribed, "April 2, '67 Vienna Jaques visited the Historian's Office and placed her autograph on this photograph." Below, the employee noted a reference to Vienna in the 4th European edition of the Doctrine and Covenants, calling page 251 a "Revelation to Vienna," referring, of course, to present-day Doctrine and Covenants section 90 given through Joseph Smith on March 8, 1833.

Two more years passed by before Vienna resurfaces in the historical record. Four years after she attended the second annual reunion, Vienna was again invited to a Zion's Camp festival on October 9, 1869, a Saturday evening after the general conference meetings that day. "The members of Zion's Camp who were in Salt Lake City held a reunion at the Social Hall."[19] Hosted by Bishop Edward Hunter, they "enjoyed in the highest degree and feelings of praise toward God and good will to men filled the hearts of those present, as they contrasted the days when the camp went up to Missouri, in the name and by command of the Lord, with the day of blessing they now enjoyed."[20] "There were also present the following persons who were driven by the mob from Jackson County, Missouri, Levi Jackman, Elijah Newman, G. W. Hancock, S. W. Brown, C. B. Hancock, and sisters Vienna Jaques, and M. E. S. Killian. One or two short addresses were delivered during the evening, and after a period of much enjoyment the party broke up with the dismissing blessing of Elder O. Hyde."[21] Vienna, now eighty-two years old, was one of approximately fifty individuals in attendance.

As a new decade began, Vienna found herself again in need of a little help from Brigham Young. She viewed Young as a man of integrity willing to help Saints in need. Brigham had demonstrated his willingness to provide counsel and to offer resolutions, not only for Vienna's past circumstances but also for the Saints at large. Brother Brigham was the person the Saints turned to when they had exhausted other options. Vienna also viewed Brigham as a resource, but one that she would only approach if absolutely necessary.

In early July 1870, she had again reached that necessity just as she had when she needed a lot of land in 1848 or when Jacob Workman overcharged her for work in 1859. This time, Vienna wrote to the Church President, "I want <to> ask you a few questions [if I can put them on paper,] I have confidence you will look on them some moment when you are at leisure, because of your willingness heretofore."[22] Vienna asked for "a load of hay" to help feed her cow after grasshoppers had destroyed her crops for the fourth time. She also informed Young that her house had been robbed of "nine gold dollors" while she was attending church one Sunday.[23] "I want to tell you that I have had a soar trial come upon me which almost made me sick," Vienna wrote. "I had my house broak open & robb[d]." Her house was ransacked three times, the robber having taken "such things as he like[d] best." The robber had bought a watch with the gold he had taken from Vienna. After she learned who the robber was ("a boy belonging to Albert Lutz"), she was able to procure the watch in an effort to regain the gold. The man from whom the robber bought the watch would not accept its return and would not return the gold to Vienna. She ran into Daniel H. Wells, Second Counselor in the First Presidency, and she turned the watch over to him to resolve the matter.[24] After insects ruined the crops she planted, and a robber took liquid capital from her home, Vienna turned to Brigham Young in her time of acute need.

No responses from Young exist on the matter of the hay, nor a resolution to the gold and watch affair. Vienna offered no further known complaint. She registered her want and told of the crime committed against her and trusted that all would be made right. For his part, Brigham generally encouraged industry, self-reliance, home manufacture, and the work of one's own hands. He encouraged the Saints to be united in doing right in temporal things.[25] Vienna abided by these principles and desired to see the Saints live up to them as well. In the end, Jaques sought out Young or other Church leaders for aid only when circumstances were unreasonable or without further recourse. Her rare letters demonstrate her independence and self-sufficient nature. They also reveal some of the everyday challenges of single womanhood in nineteenth-century Utah.

CHAPTER 15

RELIEF SOCIETY

Leaders of the Salt Lake Twelfth Ward where Vienna Jaques resided had established a Relief Society on April 29, 1868. The bishop, Leonard W. Hardy, called Priscilla Staines to serve as the president of the organization, with Amanda Barnes Smith as first counselor, Ruth Sayers as second counselor, Charlotte Payne as secretary, and Josephine Schutler as treasurer.[1] The ward was divided into nine blocks. For each block, a "teacher" was called to oversee and address the needs of the sisters residing therein.[2] Each teacher would then report to the presidency and in meetings. These leaders would work together in unity with the sisters to "search out the poor and suffering" and "as far as possible relieve the wants for all" in the ward.[3] Vienna was never called to be a teacher or to a position of leadership or responsibility in her ward.

But she did attend meetings regularly. The Twelfth Ward Relief Society typically met once a month. Vienna believed in the concept taught by Eliza R. Snow, a prominent Latter-day Saint woman charged with reestablishing the Relief Society in Utah, that the sisters should "associate together" and by doing so they would come to "love each other more" and find themselves "united and clothed with the Spirit."[4] Vienna felt the spirit of unity at the heart of Relief Society, a Zion concept to which she contributed greatly and had influence.

Vienna was in Nauvoo in 1842 for the beginnings of Relief Society, but her involvement in the organization at that time is unclear. Her name does not appear in the records of the organization from that time. The society was discontinued as the Saints prepared to go to the Rocky Mountains. It was revived for a short period in the mid-1850s. The formal reinstatement of the Relief Society came in December 1867 when Church President Brigham Young commissioned Eliza R. Snow to establish Relief Society organizations at the ward level. Young urged the women to assist the poor, to become unified as a community, and to push toward self-sufficiency.[5] During the next decade, nearly three hundred branches of the Relief Society were established throughout Utah Territory.[6] Latter-day Saint women had built a robust community for the support of others.

The restoration of the Relief Society came at a time of significant change for the people of Utah. In their messages, Church leaders increased emphasis on economic self-sufficiency, which would help against the changes wrought by outside capitalist forces—most especially the completion of the transcontinental railroad that brought new waves of non-Latter-day Saint merchants and entrepreneurs to Utah. Latter-day Saint communities under the direction of Brigham Young became more insular by directing their attention to home industry and cooperative living. At the same time, federal legislators renewed their fight to end the practice of plural marriage in Utah Territory. Amid these monumental political, economic, and cultural shifts, women played a vital role. Some stepped into the national spotlight of the public arena to promote a positive image of their faith and protect their right to practice their religion. Latter-day Saint women could speak and act collectively, but they also had individual ideas and experiences when it came to women's rights and a woman's sphere.[7]

While many operated in a broader political and economic public sphere, Vienna Jaques, like the majority of Latter-day Saint women, embraced the Relief Society, working at a local level to strengthen her community temporally and spiritually during this time of great change. Religious devotion was always at the heart of Vienna's activity in the Twelfth Ward Relief Society. She contributed theological instruction, principally on temple worship, economic egalitarianism, and home industry. She fostered unity, equality, and the building of a Zion community through the influence of her faith in word and deed.

Vienna's recorded contributions came primarily in the form of donations. She donated often. Her name can be found in most months of recorded donations to the Twelfth Ward Relief Society between January 1869 and May 1877. Often, she made donations of fruits and vegetables. She had received her land of inheritance and had put it to beneficial use. From it she grew a variety of fruits, including peaches, plums, apples, and currants, and vegetables, including peas, potatoes, squash, beans, cucumbers, and radishes.[8] She had livestock that produced milk, butter, and beef. The ever-industrious woman also donated a variety of home manufactured goods, including calico, cotton yarn, candles, soap, stockings, carpet rags, and clothing.[9] When cash was needed to help a sister purchase a sewing machine or for offerings for the poor or sick, Vienna contributed what she could.[10] This once-wealthy woman who had given all to building the kingdom of God continued to give of herself and her means to support her religious commonwealth. She endured her trials and faithfully adhered to the counsel to be economically independent and to support the poor and needy.

During June 1874, the month she turned eighty-seven years old,

Vienna wrote another letter to Brigham Young. She was apparently responding to an overture from the Church president, who had offered to send the aging sister "quarts of milk." But Vienna had no need for it this time. In fact, she had "many quarts of skim milk," which she had recently milked from her own cows. She had been donating the excess milk to poor children in her ward and she wanted to continue to do so as long as she had the "strength & resolution enough to do it." Vienna also had "a number of hundred pounds of dryed apples" on her hands and asked the Church president how she could distribute them to help others in need.[11] Vienna, it seemed, was on the lookout for opportunities to support others. Her efforts to help the poor with milk and fruit were quite timely, as a pneumonia epidemic had plagued Salt Lake City and her neighborhood during the first half of 1874.[12]

While she looked to serve the poor and needy around her, Vienna Jaques also enjoyed the camaraderie of the sisters, especially those of her ward Relief Society. Whether that meant attending to the sick, being employed in sewing or patchwork, or visiting together at a dinner party, she, like her sisters, appreciated the opportunity to dwell amid good and virtuous women, among fellow disciples.[13]

Vienna did far more than deal with temporal matters. She also provided spiritual nourishment to the sisters. She spoke when called upon to do so. Sometimes she was called upon by a leader and other times by the Spirit.

In Utah, Jaques's religious identity centered on her work in the Twelfth Ward Relief Society, where she spoke about temple ordinances, particularly those relating to spiritual work for the dead, as well as the power of prayer and the importance of properly instructing the youth. In one meeting of the Twelfth Ward Relief Society, Jaques opened the meeting with a prayer and later remarked "how very necessary it was to instruct the youth."[14] Vienna understood the importance of verbalizing and affirming the beliefs, norms, and customs of identity in the Church, for without the rising generation, a faith, a culture, and shared meanings of identity could wither away. Relief Society responsibilities had expanded in 1870 to provide guidance of teenage and young adult women.[15] On April 2, 1874, both Amanda Smith and Priscilla Staines informed the women of the Twelfth Ward that Snow had asked the ward to "organize a young ladies society."[16]

At another meeting, Jaques felt "called upon to say a few words" on the subject of prayer. Vienna was called upon to say prayers at Relief Society meetings on several occasions.[17] Her heart on this particular day in 1874 was full and though she felt to be silent, she had "a desire to encourage the young," as it pertained to the principles of prayer.[18] She stated that she had learned through her experience that prayer was most effective when she thought "to simply ask for those things which she needed." Prayer was not the only topic Vienna felt inspired to remark upon. She provided additional counsel, telling the women that they should never "be afraid to do good. you will never be sorry, don't neglect your duties. when we neglect our duties we lose. when we lose the adversary gains."[19] Vienna desired to do all the good she could.[20] She lived her life as a model of discipleship. She lived her religion and to her Relief Society sisters "bore testimony to the truth of this Latter day work." She had a reputation for possessing a passion and knowledge for scriptures.[21] Jaques remained "true to her covenants and esteemed the restoration of the Gospel as a priceless treasure."[22]

At a June 1, 1876, Relief Society meeting, Jaques remarked that her mind had "been very much occupied in regard to the Temple." At the time, the Salt Lake Temple was under construction and had been built up about twenty feet to the arches of the elongated windows on the first floor.[23] She had witnessed the tumultuous beginnings of the construction of that religious edifice since 1853. Her statement, though, did not focus on the physical construction, but on the spiritual knowledge associated with temple work. Thinking back over forty years of temple teachings, Jaques stated, "How much more we have to stimulate us than the people did in the days of the building of the Kirtland Temple. We have so much more knowledge in regard to the work to be performed therein both for the living and the dead."[24] Jaques had seen the progression and development of temples and temple ceremonies firsthand. She had contributed monetarily to the Kirtland Temple, the first temple built by the Latter-day Saints that unlocked the keys for the doctrine for baptism of the dead, and likely witnessed the dedication of the site for the Far West Temple that was never built because violence and an extermination order pushed the Church to Nauvoo. There, she witnessed and participated in the earliest baptisms for the dead before attending the Nauvoo Temple for her endowment.[25]

In a letter to Brigham Young, she stated "since the Lord has speard my life till you have commenst doing for the dead," it was her privilege now to continue to do work for her dead, for whom she claimed to have had records and information dating to the 1500s.[26] For decades Jaques had developed an understanding of the temple's importance and made every effort to share her perspective and appreciation for the ordinances performed in such a sacred space. Jaques's June 1876 statement about the knowledge the Saints had concerning baptisms for the dead came at about the same time that vicarious work, particularly endowments and sealings for the dead, was becoming a most significant aspect of Latter-day Saint temple consciousness.[27] Members like Jaques continued to develop an expanded vision of temple work, and her statement to the Relief Society indicates that she and others were making this work an even greater priority.

CHAPTER 16

At the Grove

It was about 11 a.m. on Thursday, June 8, 1876, when the eight-car train carrying Vienna and the six hundred other passengers rolled to a stop at the Provo station. The train station was located at the corner of Sixth South Street and Academy Avenue (now University Avenue) on the southern edge of the town.[1] The morning was fine, with temperatures reaching toward 80 degrees as the hundreds of passengers disembarked from the train.[2] They would have quickly walked through "one of two old ramshackle wooden depots."[3] No larger than ten people standing shoulder-to-shoulder wide and maybe twice as long, the wooden depots were little more than "cracker box stations," that were later referred to as "small and unsightly," each surrounded by a two-foot high platform.[4]

Vienna and the other excursionists were greeted there by "fifty teams of vehicles of various kinds," many of which were likely horse-drawn carts, carriages, or wagons. Provo Bishop Abraham O. Smoot and other local Church leaders had organized these vehicles to take the distinguished guests to Daniel Graves's property "located about 9th East and 8th South."[5] Graves had cultivated his land making it "a beautiful spot, with many flowers and trees and numerous statues."[6] He worked hard to make his land as comfortable as possible for the occasion. The Provo band "did good service in the musical line" as the guests arrived and boarded their next mode of conveyance en route to Graves's Park.[7]

In Provo, a "general holiday" had been declared in honor of the event. It "was a grand time" with "the stores and other places of business and schools, &c. having been closed." Great multitudes "had flocked in from some of the adjacent settlements of Utah county to give greeting and welcome to the aged fathers and mothers of Israel."[8] With a beautiful, clear blue sky and gorgeous mountains as the backdrop, Vienna and the excursionists were met by large congratulatory crowds and celebratory music. Every face was wreathed in smiles as the excursionists experienced a hero's welcoming.[9]

Arriving at the venue, Vienna would have seen the hundreds of visitors socializing as they waited for the festivities to begin. She had the entire morning's train ride to review her life's journey and think about what she might say. Just a week after she had spoken about the temple to her ward Relief Society, Vienna was ready to make another speech—this time to a much larger audience.

More than eight hundred people had gathered for the festivities at the grove. There was a "general fraternization of visitors and visited, and, at the vary large tables, arranged on purpose," a spread of food for picnics. The food disappeared quickly and "with a rapidity that suggested that age had not destroyed the relish for the good things of the earth."[10]

In the grove, Daniel Graves had erected a stand as the centerpiece of the property for the occasion. With the majestic peaks of the Wasatch Mountains serving as a magnificent background, Graves's park garden covered about one block of space with beautiful grass, flowers planted in artistic fashion, and a variety of large trees.[11] Graves and his family had lived in Provo since the mid-1850s and Daniel had developed this part of his land as a "park or resort" for events and gatherings.[12]

From the stand, Edward Hunter, Presiding Bishop of The Church of Jesus Christ of Latter-day Saints, delivered a "felicitous speech," to begin the 1876 Old Folks program to celebrate "the aged fathers and mothers of Israel."[13]

Hunter had inaugurated an Old Folks Committee the year before. Latter-day Saint photographer C. R. Savage had approached Hunter about an idea he had. While walking to work, Savage had observed an elderly woman sitting alone on her porch day after day, month after month. He assumed others lived in such a lonely existence as they aged. He approached the eighty-two-year-old Presiding Bishop about an idea for a free annual excursion for the elderly. Hunter liked the idea and assigned his sixty-year-old clerk, George Goddard, to assist with the arrangements.[14]

The first Old Folks excursion took place on May 14, 1875. All who were "seventy years old, or over, were taken by the Utah Western Railway to Dr. Clinton's Hotel, at Lake Point, on the southern shore of Great Salt Lake. Two hundred and fifty guests were entertained."[15] "Sunday school excursions, school picnics and young peoples' festivals of various kinds, are of such frequent occurrence as to excite but ordinary interest on general occasions," the *Deseret News* stated, "but a day devoted to the aged, for their especial amusement and enjoyment, has something of originality in it."[16] This innovative "old folks" celebration intrigued the local press. For example, Lula Greene Richards, editor of the *Woman's Exponent*, a periodical "central to the intellectual, religious, and social lives of many Latter-day Saint women," attended the excursion.[17] Though she was just twenty-six years old, Richards understood the importance and value of this event to honor the elderly. She declared that the "skillfully planned" excursion was "Never to be Forgotten."[18] It was, indeed, an occasion that would have staying power.

During the program portion of the festivities, "Sister Vienna Jaques, 88 years old, was called for. She gave a remarkably interesting recital of the manner in which she became acquainted with the gospel." She told the crowd about how, when living in Boston in 1831, she "read something in the paper about the 'Mormons,' and about a golden bible being found in the western part of the State of New York." Being impressed on the subject, she described how she "traveled six hundred miles to find out for herself, arriving at Kirtland, Ohio, July 4th, of the same year, and was baptised eight days afterwards." Vienna recounted the first time she met the Prophet Joseph Smith and how he "shook her by the hand and said, 'I thank God that it is given me to know when a person is honest-in-heart.'" Vienna then testified to the audience of the way she received a knowledge of the truth of the work, and of the fact of her never having doubted a moment subsequently. She further explained how she had lived to her advanced age. She did not use stimulants of any kind and had a simple diet consisting largely of milk. Vienna emphasized as she closed her remarks that she had lived in the Lord, and "when she died she wanted to die in the Lord."[19]

Vienna was the concluding speaker at the inaugural Old Folks Day. Following her remarks, "most of the company" boarded the steamboat *City of Corinne* and enjoyed a sail with a gentle breeze on the Great Salt Lake. It is reported that the guests were "royally entertained." People, their countenances radiant with pleasure, engaged in reciting to each other the events of by-gone days.[20]

Those radiant countenances were found again in Graves's grove in Provo on June 8, 1876, for the Second Annual Old Folks Day. The Church's Presiding Bishop Edward Hunter gave a congratulatory speech to open the program. George Goddard followed "in the same agreeable strain."[21] An aged couple, "Father Vincent, aged 102 years" and "his faithful wife, Mother Vincent, aged 99," each made a few remarks. Mother Vincent "said she had lived thirty years with her respected partner without having once seen the brightness of his countenance shadowed by a frown."[22] "Brother W. C. Dunbar sang, in his most felicitous and inimitable style, with appropriate gestures, attitude, voice, and tone, 'My Dear Old Wife and I,' which took immensely, the surrounding circumstances giving it more than usual effect. Then followed an impressive scene, when, in the presence of that large assemblage, Elders Taylor, Woodruff and Pratt pronounced, by virtue of the Priesthood, a blessing upon the heads of the aged couple, Father and Mother Vincent."[23] Vienna was next.

What did she say to the crowd gathered that warm day of June 8, 1876, in Provo?

It is a bit of a mystery. She could have talked about anything from her life or forty-five years' experience in the church. From available, known historical accounts we only know that she "gave an interesting account of some of her early experience in connection with the Church."[24]

As she stood in front of the hundreds of attendees at the grove in Provo, any number of Vienna's stories would have enraptured the audience. She could have described her witness and testimony of the Book of Mormon that took her on a solo journey from Boston to Kirtland, Ohio, where she was baptized into the new faith. She could have talked about meeting Joseph Smith for the first time. She could have given the details of spreading the gospel message with Samuel Smith and Orson Hyde. She could have talked about helping her sister flee to Zion. She could have given particulars about her immense donation that helped the Church move forward with building the Kirtland Temple. She could have depicted the horrors of the violence she witnessed in Missouri and the letter of comfort she received from the Prophet that was an answer to her prayers in that most difficult and trying time. She could have given insights to the first baptism for the dead and her experiences in the Nauvoo Temple. Any of these accounts would have been inspiring to hear.

We don't know exactly what Vienna Jaques said that day. We do know that as a female landowner who was building considerable wealth on the east coast of the United States, Vienna Jaques would stand out in any historical consideration of nineteenth-century America. But, because she converted to the restored gospel of Jesus Christ, she took the same characteristics and personality traits that made her unusual in Boston and Providence and brought them to bear on the destiny of The Church of Jesus Christ of Latter-day Saints. Vienna's life was shaped by the Church, and she in turn helped shape the Church in a few pivotal moments.

Vienna was again the event's closing speaker. Following her remarks, the attendees "dispersed, some to the dance, others to the swing, and many seated under the shady trees talking over the reminiscences of the past." Before long, as the afternoon reached toward evening, the excursionists loaded into the same vehicles that conveyed them to the grove. They arrived at the station and boarded the Utah Southern train headed back north to Salt Lake City, departing about 4:30 p.m. Of the return trip, George Goddard stated, "On our way home, cakes and lemonade were handed to every one in each Car, and after that, a song by 7th Ward band, in every car." The ride took about two and a half hours; Vienna and the rest of the aged excursionists arrived at the depot in Salt Lake City about 7:00 p.m.[25]

"On the entire trip, from starting to return," the *Deseret News* reported, "we have not heard of anything that occurred to mar the enjoyment of the affair, and it will be a time likely to be cherished in the memories of those who participated."[26] "Thus terminated," Old Folks Committee member

George Goddard confided to his journal, "one of the most enjoyable associations & excursions that ever took place in Salt Lake City."[27] Goddard continued, "I was very much exhausted having devoted constant attention to the happiness of the excursionists." That exhaustion continued to the next day and kept Goddard "very tired and weary from yesterdays exertions."[28] Imagine how Vienna Jaques must have felt being nearly thirty years Goddard's senior. Though tired from the excursion, Vienna surely would have mustered the strength to celebrate her eighty-ninth birthday two days later on June 10.

According to the *Deseret News*, the excursion to Provo "was one of the most interesting affairs of the kind which ever took place in Utah."[29] After driving a wagon team across the plains almost twenty-five years earlier, Jaques was likely thrilled by the train's ability to travel more than one hundred miles in a day.[30] A trip that would have taken days each way was accomplished in mere hours. And the respect shown to Vienna and other Church veterans demonstrates the reverence and celebration with which the Saints regarded their hard-won sacrifices.[31]

Old Folks Day became something of a movement in Utah communities and even extended to neighboring states. Similar entertainments were provided annually. The yearly gatherings were considered "most novel and interesting" with "few if any parallels anywhere."[32] The Latter-day Saint initiative was a significant and sustained effort to ensure "the aged everywhere, irrespective of age, color or religious persuasion, are the recipients of public favor and consideration."[33] The summer excursions were extraordinary and the committee eventually added theatrical entertainments for the aged in the winter as well.

These efforts evince the respect and reverence for the aged and a desire within the Latter-day Saint community to "honor those who came before and bestow kindly attention on them while they are alive."[34] The efforts made to celebrate the elderly offered an impressive demonstration of devotion and commitment that was forged in the difficulties of the Church's first fifty years, especially the trek west. Those that had been part of the Latter-day Saint faith since its early days were honored for their efforts, desires, and choices to make the sacrifices for the fervor of their faith.

During decades when Latter-day Saints were under intense external pressure, especially from the federal government trying to eradicate plural marriage, these commemorative occasions served to affirm community solidarity. As the first generation of Latter-day Saints was beginning to pass on and most of the younger generation had no personal experience or memory of the founding events of the community, these memorial events were an exercise in community affirmation and transmission. They heard directly from the old folks, who had experienced decades of trials, their "expressions of trust in God and unshaken faith in the Gospel."[35]

Old age was (and is) part of the fabric of everyday life. Respect for old age and the contributions of these veterans was manifest among nineteenth-century Latter-day Saints. Joseph Smith modeled the reverence of old age. In May 1843, he taught, "The way to get along in any important matters was to gather unto yourself wise men, experienced & aged men to assist in council."[36] Age and experience provided wisdom and counsel. This was a Christian value that adhered to Protestant ideals.[37] It aligned with a passage from Proverbs: "The hoary head is a crown of glory, if it be found in the way of righteousness."[38] Perhaps Wilford Woodruff had that scripture in mind when he drew a crown in his journal alongside a train as he penned an entry following the June 8, 1876, Old Folks excursion to Provo.[39]

Vienna attended subsequent Old Folks events. She is mentioned as being present on June 24, 1879, at the Fifth Annual Old Folks Excursion. That year, more than six hundred people thronged an eleven-car train to convey the old folks to American Fork.[40] They left Salt Lake City at 7:30 a.m. and arrived at their destination a couple of hours later.

The *Deseret News* described the scene: "The weather was glorious, everybody was in high spirits and the orchards and farms which adorned the landscape on either side of the track looked fresh and bright and beautiful in the glowing sunlight."[41] Seemingly the whole town showed up for the party. Children lined the road and greeted the aged visitors with cheers and songs. Young women and young men decorated a platform with flowers and boughs. There was plenty of food to go along with the music, orations, games, and prizes.

Vienna was presented with a bouquet bestowed upon her by some of the little girls. She was the oldest woman named in attendance that day, having reached ninety-two years.[42] If she were in fact the oldest woman in attendance, she would have been gifted a "handsome arm chair" given to "the oldest lady present."[43]

Vienna would have listened as eighty-six-year-old Edward Hunter spoke about religious liberty. Hunter "lamented the fact that the religious liberty for which the fathers bled had been denied to the Latter-day Saints . . . He prophesied that this liberty denied would yet be obtained, and we would extend it to all nations and religions without exception. He viewed with joy the prospect of his approaching departure to a better world, blessed those present, and exhorted all to continued faith and obedience."[44] Vienna also would have heard the compelling stories of Mary Shelley, then eighty-three years old, who had worked forty years in the coal mines of Scotland and had crossed the plains. She told of an incident when she was bitten by a rattlesnake on the plains and was healed through the laying on of hands by the elders.[45] The orations that day demonstrated trust in God and unwavering faith in the gospel of Jesus Christ. Good feelings prevailed, and affection, friendship, and unity were exhibited—the feeling of Zion. Of the event, the *Deseret News* concluded, "God bless the aged of Israel and give them joy and peace to the end of their earthly career."[46]

Up until this time, old age did not seem to be slowing Vienna Jaques down. Just two weeks before the Fifth Annual Old Folks excursion, she celebrated her ninety-second birthday. Some sisters, likely from her Twelfth Ward Relief Society, surprised Vienna at her home on Tuesday, June 10, 1879. These unnamed sisters brought with them "a bountiful supply of good things for the table, to celebrate" their aged sister. The company enjoyed themselves in conversation and reading together.[47]

As Vienna had lived through and was so "well versed in the early history of the Church, she rehearsed for their benefit many incidents that were interesting" to the women present. Among the items she read to them was "a letter of four pages written to her by the Prophet Joseph." The letter Jaques shared that day may have been the September 4, 1833, letter Joseph Smith wrote to her during the height of difficulty the Saints experienced in Jackson County, Missouri. That letter had three pages of text and a fourth that contained addressing. If it was that letter, she likely had a copy of it made before she donated the original letter to the Church Historian's Office decades earlier. Regardless of whether it was that letter or another unknown letter that Joseph may have written to Vienna, the seasoned sister felt impressed to share her history with the women who had come to celebrate her in her old age.[48]

Being a veteran of the Church became something of an occupation for Vienna. She attended and even spoke at many events honoring longtime faithful Church members. These events featured the aged to serve as "living links to the past, reminding younger generations of persons and experiences, good and bad, which they would never know except through the communication of others."[49] The celebrations of the aged also functioned as occasions for the participants themselves to affirm their faith as they faced the end of their mortal lives.

As Vienna persevered in life, she treasured her history and the words of the Prophet. Perhaps knowing that her long life would soon reach its conclusion, she took every opportunity to share her experience, wisdom, and faith with any audience willing to listen.

CHAPTER 17

Final Days in Salt Lake City

Eight days before Vienna's ninety-third birthday, a census taker named Howland V. Stevenson knocked on her door. He was in Salt Lake City's Twelfth Ward to compile data for the federal government about the inhabitants. Based on a constitutional mandate, the census is taken every ten years and asks questions, including how many people live or stay in each home, and the sex, age, and race of each person in the home to get an accurate count of people in each town and city.

Stevenson briefly interviewed Vienna and recorded her statistics. She was counted as the head of a household that also included Philip Huett, a seventy-six-year-old divorced man who worked as a gardener. Stevenson listed Vienna as widowed; Daniel Shearer, her estranged husband, had died six years earlier, though they had not lived together for decades. The census taker listed Vienna's occupation as "keeping house."[1] According to the census's instructions, "Women keeping house for their own families or for themselves, without any other gainful occupation, will be entered as 'keeping house.'"[2] The snapshot Stevenson captured of Vienna's life in the census that early June day resembled the life she had led for at least the previous fifty years: industriously taking care of her home and others in need.

Vienna's name appears infrequently in just a few historical sources during her waning years. These included the *Woman's Exponent*, a paper dedicated to the "Rights of the Women of Zion, and the Rights of the Women of all Nations." Romania B. Pratt, the first Latter-day Saint woman to earn a medical degree, had returned to Salt Lake City from Boston by 1880 to train women in medicine and midwifery. She authored a brief article entitled, "Birthday Anniversary of One of Our Oldest Veterans." Romania had gone with a "few friends" to the "house of our old and long tried friend" to congratulate and celebrate the birthday of Vienna Jaques on June 10, 1880, the week following her visit from the census taker.[3] "The old lady's apparent lease of life and vigor is remarkable still and bids fair to give us all the rare privilege of beholding one having lived an hundred years," Romania wrote with admiration. The doctor continued her report to the *Woman's Exponent*, describing Vienna's physical appearance: "The erectness of her carriage is sufficient to fill many of the Misses of the nineteenth century with envy. May she live as long as she desires, and may the angel of the Lord preserve her from all evil both seen and unseen is the prayer of all her numerous friends."[4]

Several times as she inched up in age the community feted Vienna Jaques on her birthday.[5] In addition to the birthday parties, Jaques was among those invited to attend the yearly anniversary dinners celebrating the birth of Joseph Smith and was mentioned as among the living veterans of the violent Jackson County, Missouri, expulsion nearly fifty years earlier. By this point, Vienna was among fewer than one hundred other named Latter-day Saints "who were in Jackson County and who are still alive." That was equal to less than 10 percent of the Latter-day Saints that had lived in Jackson County fifty years earlier, and many of those listed had been children or less than twenty years old when the Saints were driven from their homes in 1833.[6]

On December 23, 1880, the anniversary of the birth of the Prophet Joseph Smith, Vienna attended the celebration with "many of his old friends and members of his family, and others who revere his memory."[7] A sumptuous supper was provided for the partygoers "at the former residence of Bro. Shadrach Roundy." Vienna sat at the table alongside such persons as John Taylor (who had officially become the third President of the Church in October of that year), Joseph F. Smith, Wilford Woodruff, Phoebe Woodruff, Patty Sessions, Presendia L. Kimball, Mercy R. Thompson, Emmeline B. Wells, and Bathsheba W. Smith.

The attendees heard speeches on Joseph's teachings and remarks from current Church leaders, John Taylor, Joseph F. Smith, and Wilford Woodruff. They also enjoyed hearing readings of major addresses that the Prophet had reportedly given, such as the Appeal to the Green Mountain Boys in 1843 and his last words to the Nauvoo Legion.[8] Partygoers also experienced singing, readings of history and poetry about the Prophet, and an ornamented birthday cake. The party lasted five hours. According to the *Deseret News*, "The party was an exceedingly happy and pleasant one. Many old veterans were there and participated in the enjoyment." The event honored the Prophet Joseph Smith and ensured that those in attendance and those who would read about the festivities in the newspaper remembered him as "one of the grandest, noblest men, who ever lived."[9]

"This is probably the first affair of its kind yet inaugurated," the *Deseret News* said of the event honoring Joseph Smith's birth. The newspaper encouraged Latter-day Saints everywhere to celebrate and commemorate: "We should be pleased to see the custom perpetuated, each ward taking its annual turn in doing honor to the memory of the great and glorious Prophet, Joseph Smith."[10] As the first generation of Latter-day Saints were reaching their twilight years, it became increasingly important for them to hold these and other events to cement their experiences, memories, and history into the hearts and minds of the younger generations. Doing so helped form a collective memory about the early years of the Church, its members, and the first prophet of the latter-day dispensation. They passed on their knowledge and testimonies to the rising generations, who would come to understand clearly where they had come from and what they had experienced for their faith. The rising generations would then, it was hoped, perpetuate and strengthen that collective memory.

While the people of Utah celebrated and honored Jaques for her stalwart faith, her sacrifices, and her veteran status in the Church during the last decade of her life, Jaques's health began to fade. On the morning of April 23, 1881, she suffered a serious fall and broke her hip. She was taken to the Church president's office, where John Taylor and Wilford Woodruff administered to her. They gave her a priesthood blessing, anointing her head with oil to aid in the healing process. These brethren spent the better part of that morning administering to Sister Jaques.[11] Historical records do not disclose the outcome of her health travails at that time.

Perhaps as she recuperated, she began to consider the long-term implications of and preservation for some things she held dear. In her modest home she had a treasure trove of Church history artifacts. Among them was a "cloak belonging to the Prophet Joseph Smith." It was a heavy blue cloak with a green wool liner tailored for him by John A. Bills, a general in the Nauvoo Legion in charge of quartermaster, or the person responsible for providing clothing and supplies, among other needs.[12] How she acquired it is unknown, but it was an item with a tangible connection to Joseph. Vienna contacted Joseph L. Barfoot, the manager and curator of the Deseret Museum.[13] Through Barfoot, she donated the cloak to the museum. Vienna gave up her corporeal connection to Joseph Smith, but doing so would keep his memory alive among the Saints by giving them a tactile piece from the Prophet's life.[14] Upon receiving the donation, Barfoot contacted Wilford Woodruff via letter and then took the cloak to show it to the President of the Quorum of the Twelve Apostles.[15]

As the year 1881 ended, Vienna made arrangements for the most cherished of her property: the land of her inheritance. She had settled, tilled, and improved this lot of land for more than thirty years. In fulfillment of revelation, she had lived a life of faith and resided on her land of inheritance in relative peace. On the last day of December 1881, at the age of ninety-four, she signed an agreement to sell her lot of land to Joseph F. Smith, then the Second Counselor in the Church's First Presidency. Smith gave Jaques $3,000 for the deed to the land, which Jaques signed. Jaques's real estate had been valued at $2,000 ten years earlier during the 1870 census.[16] The uncertain strokes of her signature reveal a hand trembling with age and frailty.[17]

According to the agreement, Smith would "provide food, clothing, fuel and all other things that may be necessary for the comfortable support of the said party of the second part during the term of her natural life, and at her demise to pay, or to cause to be paid the expenses incidental to her funeral and internment."[18] Furthermore, the agreement allowed Jaques to remain in her house for the low rent of five dollars per year. It appears that Jaques made this agreement to ensure that she would be provided for during the last years of her life. Though she spent much of her life caring for others, this was perhaps the first time that she truly felt that she needed someone else to care for her. The Church held on to her land for the next five years, three years beyond her final days on earth.[19]

Months later, in 1882 the aging woman was again treated to a surprise party for her ninety-fifth birthday anniversary.[20] A "goodly number of 'Ye old-time friends' of Mrs. Vienna Jaques, who is quite a historical personage and well-known in this community," assembled at her residence on the afternoon of June 10. An impromptu bowery was speedily erected covering tables filled with a variety of gourmet foods "attractive enough to tempt a[n] epicuere."[21] According to the *Salt Lake Herald*'s report of Jaques's ninety-fifth birthday celebration, "Music, speeches and an original poem by Mrs. Julia Wennerholm enlivened the occasion." The "ancient dame," as she was labeled by the newspaper, "was looking her very best, and who was seated at the head of the table received the honors with the becoming dignity of a lady of the old school of a past century." At this, her last reported birthday party, the *Herald* noted, "A cheerful and peaceful spirit prevailed and after enjoying a happy season the party separated, wishing that her life's 'late afternoon, where, cool and long the shadows grow,' may be as serene as was that tranquil evening."[22]

Unfortunately for Vienna Jaques, the woman who faced a series of tremendous hardships with faith and determination to build Zion, tranquility would not be the word to characterize the end of her life. She became very weak both in body and mind. Her mind started to deteriorate. Vienna's mental capacity and cognition became such that "that she would ramble in her speech," which became "incoherent and utterly irresponsible." Alongside her mental decline, eventually Vienna became physically bedridden, unable to help herself in any way.[23]

Only when the effects of an accident, an undisclosed mental malady (probably dementia), and old age began to overtake her did the consummate independent woman lean on neighbors, friends, and the Relief Society for help.[24] Vienna had spent her whole life working industriously and helping others. Now, the self-reliant soul had become totally reliant on others. A little over two years after she signed the agreement with Smith for her land of inheritance, Vienna Jaques's infirm body gave way in her home early on the morning of February 7, 1884. She was ninety-six years old.

CHAPTER 18

Laid to Rest

At 10:30 a.m. on Sunday, February 10, 1884, many friends and neighbors gathered at the Salt Lake City Twelfth Ward meetinghouse for the funeral services of the widely respected Vienna Jaques. She had been gone just three days when they met to celebrate her "life-long integrity" and "strength of character."[1] The congregation sat reverently listening to the speakers, which included Wilford Woodruff (then President of the Quorum of the Twelve Apostles), Heber J. Grant (then a member of the Quorum of the Twelve Apostles), Charles W. Penrose (then a counselor in the Salt Lake Stake Presidency), and George Hamlin (who wrote Vienna's obituary).[2]

Woodruff was the service's concluding speaker. For thirty minutes he gave "instructive and consolatory" remarks about the life of the dearly departed sister. The President of the Twelve waxed poetic about "the integrity and liberality of the deceased." He then talked about the last few months of Vienna's life. He described how her body had become feeble, and her mind had become so much affected that her speech became "totally irresponsible." He informed the audience "that she was not accountable for things she had said during her last illness, and could not be blamed for them."³ Her death was considered "a happy release from pain and weakness."⁴ President Woodruff's words rightfully honored the sacrificing, service-oriented, Zion-building, faithful Latter-day Saint. In his journal that day, Woodruff drew a small, ornamented coffin devoted to "Vienna Jaques 96."⁵

In addition to hearing good words from the cadre of speakers, the Twelfth Ward choir sang a beautiful selection of music to pay tribute to Jaques, their departed ward member. "Their singing was quite a noticeable feature of the services," the *Deseret News* remarked. Then her remains were taken to the Salt Lake City Cemetery for burial."⁶ There in the frozen ground of the south-central area of the cemetery, Vienna Jaques was laid to rest. Eventually, a small, unassuming gravestone was placed to mark her final resting place.

An obituary for Vienna appeared on the front page of the February 13 issue of the *Deseret News*. The two-paragraph article offered praiseworthy words about the "aged veteran," characterizing her as a virtuous woman and a historic figure. Like Woodruff had in his funerary commentary, the obituary remarked on the loss of her mental powers and the health travails Vienna passed through during the final stage of her life.

Nearly three weeks later, in the pages of the *Woman's Exponent*, another, more in-depth obituary written by George Hamlin appeared. How Hamlin came to befriend Vienna is not known. Hamlin was born in Boston, Massachusetts, in 1821; perhaps his family became acquainted with Vienna when she also lived in the old Puritan city there in the 1820s and early 1830s. Hamlin seems to have known a great deal about Vienna, especially her early history. His memorial focused on her early life, conversion to the restored gospel, and the verses of revelation that named her.⁷

Hamlin then summarized an eventful life. He noted that Vienna had "passed through the early trials and persecutions, and finally, with the exodus from Nauvoo, drove her own team across the plains and settled on the lot which was apportioned to her in the 12th Ward of this city." "She was a person of marked individuality of character," Hamlin wrote, "yet with all her peculiarity of temperament she was true to her covenants and esteemed the restoration of the Gospel as a priceless treasure." Hamlin concluded by asking readers to have grace for the way Vienna's life finished. "Toward the close of her life," Hamlin stated, "owing to intense suffering consequent upon an accident and extreme old age, her mental faculties were clouded and her speech quite incoherent. Let us be charitable to the weakness of frail mortality." Hamlin finished the obituary with this poem:

> *He who knows our frame is just,*
> *Merciful, and compassionate,*
> *And full of sweet assurance*
> *And hope for all, the language is,*
> *That He remembereth we are dust.*[8]

Vienna Jaques was remembered as a woman of faith, strong "in the principles of the Gospel," and liberal in her dealings with others.[9] She was an independent pioneer, a caregiver who selflessly served others. She was fearless in spirit and a champion of righteousness. She led a life of noble influence and was an enduring inspiration to those who knew her. She led a life of exemplary discipleship.

Vienna Jaques's gravesite was hidden in the shadow of a massive monument to Orson Pratt, who had died two and a half years earlier in October 1881. At some point, probably decades after her death, the small, unassuming gravestone placed at Vienna's gravesite was replaced by another modest marker. Why a replacement was necessary is not known. The new gravestone read: "Vienna Jaques 1833–1884." The writing inscribed on this gravestone is incorrect. Vienna Jaques was born on June 10, 1787, not in 1833. The year 1833, however, is an important date for Latter-day Saints and historians' views of Vienna. That year, on March 8, she was named by the Lord in one of Joseph Smith's revelations; she remains one of only two women mentioned by name in the canonized revelations of The Church of Jesus Christ of Latter-day Saints, the other being Emma Smith. The gravestone, however, was a misrepresentation of Vienna's life; one that was literally etched in stone.

The barely noticeable, non-descript gravestone belies the fascinating life of Vienna Jaques. Her position in the cemetery, especially when juxtaposed against the massive Orson Pratt marker, is perhaps a metaphor for a deficiency in the number of pages and stories told about female and lesser-known Church members. Orson Pratt was certainly an important figure, but so was Vienna Jaques. She was a unique figure and simultaneously representative of the general Latter-day Saint experience. Jaques and others like her deserve to have their history told and their lives and contributions remembered. Their individual choices influence our own understanding of the nature of religion and religious identity in the nineteenth century, and just how contingent, evolving, and occasionally limiting that identity was. Jaques's life gives us insight into those choices and into the power of religious identity and consciousness. Her history also illuminates the role and place of women in Latter-day Saint society and economy, and therefore provides a useful lens through which to view the first half-century of not only Church history, but also the first thirty-plus years of Utah territorial history.

For most who know her name, Jaques was a woman who sacrificed much for her faith, though her name is typically only acknowledged in reference to a significant financial donation she made to the Church around 1833 or as a possible plural wife of Joseph Smith. Jaques's life, however, was much more, although that life has largely been lost to history. Her history, her independence, her resourcefulness, her assertiveness, and her generosity deserve our attention even if she was not a prominent person from a prominent family or in any position of authority. Her life teaches that though not everyone can be in a position of leadership, everyone can display the leadership principles of discipleship. All can be leaders in their own sphere of influence: in organizing and conducting charitable acts and in building Zion in everyday life. It is, after all, the everyday living of faith that is truly heroic. It is the everyday contributions that build toward the extraordinary.

POSTLUDE

Salt Lake City Cemetery

My journey getting to know Vienna Jaques began in 2012. I was working on the third volume of the Documents series of the Joseph Smith Papers. One of the documents I was assigned to work on was the September 4, 1833, letter Joseph Smith wrote to Vienna. She had treasured that letter; I felt honored for the opportunity to study the text and investigate the context surrounding this letter.

I was quickly captivated by what I learned about Vienna Jaques. I was surprised and disappointed to find that few parts of Vienna's life story had been mentioned in the writing of Doctrine and Covenants commentaries or in the telling of Church history. They usually told the same simplistic story that Vienna, a wealthy woman, had been commanded to consecrate her means to the Church and she went on to live a long, faithful life. As I researched the many facets of that September 1833 letter and uncovered sources that I hadn't seen cited elsewhere, I knew there was more to say about Vienna Jaques and her history.

Given the constraints of the Joseph Smith Papers Project, I could not include all the research I had compiled into Documents Volume 3. I had an opportunity to build on that research and continue it, determined to publish an article about her. It turned out I got two opportunities to write about Vienna: one was an article for the *Ensign* and the second a scholarly article for what was then titled *Mormon Historical Studies* (now *Latter-day Saint Historical Studies*).[1]

It was during the process of writing these two articles that I first went to the Salt Lake City Cemetery to visit Vienna's gravesite. Upon arriving and finding the stone that marked her resting place, I noticed immediately that her birth year was incorrect. I was upset. How could this mistake have been made? How could someone I found so fascinating be forgotten so much that a wildly inaccurate birth year was engraved into her headstone? I felt I needed to do something to help others get to know Vienna Jaques. I was already drafting the articles, but I also took many opportunities to speak about her in formal speeches, in interviews, in lessons, in firesides, and in informal conversations.

I began to go each year to the cemetery to pay my respects. Each year on, or near, her birthday, I made the trip to the Salt Lake City Cemetery. Each year as the spring hits full bloom so do the rosebushes on the south side of my house. Beautiful yellow and peach colored roses grow in abundance on these bushes. Each June, I cut a handful of these roses and take them with me to the cemetery. The yellow roses symbolize a friendship that has grown, and the peach roses convey my sense of gratitude to Vienna for what her life of discipleship has taught me. I continue to make annual visits to the cemetery.

In 2015 and 2016, I published the two articles I had been working on. I thought that my work on Vienna was complete. By happenstance, I continued to find new bits and pieces of information about Vienna. Whenever I found something about her, I would put it into a file. There didn't seem to be enough to write anything new. But over the course of another six years, I had compiled a hefty file.

Vienna was on my mind when I was in Logan, Utah, on June 3, 2022, for the Mormon History Association Conference. That night, sitting in my hotel room alone with my thoughts, I wondered if I had enough new material to write another article. Or maybe I could combine the new research with the old and write a book? Quickly, I sketched out what a book-length biography might look like. By early the next morning, I had written an outline. A week later, I took four yellow and peach roses to the cemetery.

In the months that followed, I organized the research I had accumulated over the previous ten years and determined where I still needed to look. More new finds and more organizing. A biography was beginning to take shape.

On Saturday, October 22, 2022, I attended the rededication ceremony of the Brigham Young Family Cemetery in downtown Salt Lake City. At that event, I had the opportunity to visit with Kim R. Wilson, chair of the Ensign Peak Foundation (an organization dedicated to preserving "the rich heritage associated with The Church of Jesus Christ of Latter-day Saints"). Kim notified me that his foundation had recently placed a new marker at Vienna Jaques's gravesite. I was thrilled and profoundly grateful. The day was a bit cold and drizzly, but I rushed over to the Salt Lake City Cemetery to see it. I thought it was a beautiful, befitting monument to Vienna. The devoted disciple now had an accurate and dignified headstone.

A press of business and other responsibilities prevented me from working on the biography as winter came and went. Spring 2023 was in full bloom. It was time to go to the cemetery.

I had a business trip that conflicted with Vienna's birthday, so I went on June 7, 2023. Crouching near her headstone that day, I felt an urgency to get to work. From that time, every free moment I had, I dedicated myself to working on Vienna's biography. I wrote two chapters while on the business trip that weekend. By the end of June, I had four chapters. It became something of a compulsion, but the words seemed to flow together as I finished chapter after chapter. By November, I had seventeen chapters drafted, and before long the manuscript was completed.

I have long felt a connection to Vienna Jaques. The more I have come to know her, the more I have wanted others to know her as well. Perhaps some of that came as I cared for my own grandmother during her health travails, her battle with dementia, and her ultimate death. As I cared for my grandmother (a strong, independent woman in her own right) from February 2023 through January 2024, I felt my connection to Vienna and her history grow even stronger.

Vienna Jaques's whole history has never been told before. Though she is mentioned by name in the Doctrine and Covenants, Vienna Jaques was not a prominent woman in the Church. Neither did she leave behind much of a documentary record. Beyond bits and pieces of documentation about locations where she lived, little is known of Vienna's first forty years of life. She did not keep a diary or write a memoir. In fact, she produced few surviving documents, and her name is mentioned in letters, journals, newspapers, and other documents only sporadically in her nearly ninety-seven years of life. With just these strands of a variety of sources woven together to form an imperfect and incomplete tapestry, this biography has attempted to reconstruct highlights from Vienna's life, but it cannot reconstruct her voice. Her voice is her own and it is largely lost to history. Yet it emerges in timely places and is ultimately heard in the eternities.

Uncovering her past has been a challenging decade-long process that required a deep level of investigative sleuthing into a wide variety of records of the past. What has emerged from this investigation are fascinating insights into a single woman's experience during the first fifty years of The Church of Jesus Christ of Latter-day Saints. A woman who was an eyewitness to some of the most challenging and inspiring times of the Restoration.

This history has centered on Vienna's experiences in New England, conversion to the restored gospel of Jesus Christ, consecration of substantial means to the Church, expulsion from a variety of gathering places, efforts to build Zion, witnessing of the first baptism for the dead and subsequent ordinance work for deceased peoples, trek to the Salt Lake Valley, service in the Relief Society, teaching to the rising generations, life in the first decades of settlement in the Salt Lake Valley, and ultimate battle with dementia and death. Vienna lived a life that was both everyday and extraordinary.

Her story deserves an audience as large and broad as possible that they may learn from her the power of conversion, sacrifice, and faith. It has been an honor to get to know Vienna Jaques and to tell her story. I only hope I have done her life and history the justice she deserves.

Acknowledgments

During the creation, development, and production of any book, every author accumulates many personal debts. A simple thank-you here feels terribly inadequate, though I hope this list helps alleviate some of the debts I owe.

Over the years many historians, editors, librarians, archivists, and other professionals in the historians' community have assisted me in locating historical sources for and thinking through the writing (and revising) of the narrative of this biography. Among those who have especially supported me on this book, I extend my gratitude to (in alphabetical order by last name): Mark Ashurst-McGee, Ron Barney, Gerrit Dirkmaat, Brett Dowdle, Ron Esplin, Anna Graff, David Grua, Christian Heimburger, Sharalyn Howcroft, Robin Jensen, Brooke Jurges, Chase Kirkham, Elizabeth Kuehn, Riley Lorimer, Jeffrey Mahas, Alan Morrell, Sharon Nielsen, Ardis Parshall, Adam Petty, Brenden Rensink, Alex Smith, R. Eric Smith, Jenny Reeder, and Emily Utt.

When I completed a draft of the book, a handful of dedicated scholars agreed to read and comment on the manuscript. Matthew C. Godfrey,

ACKNOWLEDGMENTS

Claire Haynie, Spencer W. McBride, Matthew S. McBride, and Lisa Olsen Tait offered terrific notes and observations that helped me rethink and rewrite portions of the manuscript. Their careful reading and commentary helped me to improve the presentation of this biography. To each of them, I am most indebted.

I approached Janiece Johnson of Deseret Book in September 2023 to gauge her interest in this biography. Janiece expressed immediate enthusiasm and has been an incredible advocate for it ever since. She also read the entire manuscript and offered incisive insights. Thank you, Janiece! I am grateful to Kristen Evans for her excellent editorial eye. I am thankful that this biography is even better than it would have otherwise been because of her work. Other staff members at Deseret Book, including Garth Bruner, Halle Ballingham, and Rachael Ward, have likewise been wonderful to work with. I deeply appreciate all who have labored to help me get this book published!

To my friends and neighbors in the Farmington Bay 8th Ward, your love and support has often sustained me. Thank you for your collective goodness!

The biggest debt is always owed to the people closest to the author. They take the brunt of the time, energy, and effort the author spends away from attending to responsibilities and relationships in order to focus on producing the book. Ashley, Keagan, Makinsey, and Braxton, I love you all! I know how much each of you contributed, and how much each of you sacrificed, so that I could research, write, and ultimately publish this book. I will never forget it and will be eternally grateful. Many other dear friends and family members provided a multitude of support and/or a listening ear when I needed it. I hope you all know how much you mean to me.

This book is dedicated to the lives and memories of my grandmother

ACKNOWLEDGMENTS

and father, both of whom departed this life within three months of each other as I was completing this book. My words fail when I think of the incalculable ways they have shaped my life. But I am who I am, in no small part, because of them.

Notes

PRELUDE: UTAH CENTRAL DEPOT–SALT LAKE CITY

1. "A Gay Excursion Party," *Deseret News*, 21 June 1876.
2. "A Gay Excursion Party," *Deseret News*.
3. "A Gay Excursion Party"; Wilford Woodruff, Journal, 8 June 1876, CHL.
4. "A Gay Excursion Party," *Deseret News*.
5. "A Gay Excursion Party," *Deseret News*.
6. "A Gay Excursion Party," *Deseret News*.

CHAPTER 1: EARLY DAYS IN NEW ENGLAND

1. Massachusetts, Births, 1636–1924, *FamilySearch*.
2. George Hamlin, "In Memoriam," *Woman's Exponent* 12, no. 19 (1 March 1884): 152; Joseph Lemuel Chester, *John Rogers: The Compiler of the First Authorised English Bible* (London: Longman, Green, Longman, and Roberts, 1861).
3. This information was obtained from *FamilySearch* records. There is a "Spencer Jaques" listed as Vienna's brother in the baptisms for the dead register. Corresponding sources to verify another brother have not been located.
4. Department of Commerce and Labor, Bureau of the Census, S.N.D. North, Director, *Heads of Families at the First Census of the United States taken in the Year 1790: Massachusetts* (Washington: Government Printing Office, 1908), 9.
5. Duane Hamilton Hurd, *History of Essex County, Massachusetts* (Philadelphia: J.W. Lewis & Co., 1888), 675.
6. By 1790, Henry was listed as a head of household in Newbury (the town of his birth) about eighteen miles north of Beverly, and thereafter, Vienna had connections

NOTES

to Georgetown and Rowley—both places in the same county located between Beverly and Newbury. *Heads of Families at the First Census of the United States*, 86.

7. Nancy F. Cott, *The Bonds of Womanhood: "Woman's Sphere" in New England, 1780–1835* (New Haven, CT: Yale University Press, 1977), 19–62, 127–159.

8. Robert A. McCaughey, "From Town to City: Boston in the 1820s," *Political Science Quarterly* 88, no. 2 (June 1973): 191, 194.

9. The era's advancing industrial revolution spurred growth in manufacturing. The infusion of capital from war profits and an increase of import and export trade to and from the city further increased growth. Factories, mills, manufacturing, shipbuilding, and construction projects exploded in Boston during the early nineteenth century. The city became both a permanent and temporary destination and jumping off point for jobs both in the city and in outlying areas. Grappling with this rapid change, the city government provided professionalized municipal services and kept the streets clean. McCaughey, "From Town to City," 203, 207; Edward L. Glaeser, "Reinventing Boston: 1640–2003," Working Paper 10166, NBER Working Paper Series, National Bureau of Economic Research, (Cambridge, MA: December 2003); S.E. Morison, *The Maritime History of Massachusetts* (Boston: Northeastern University Press, 1961); Peter Temin, *Engines of Enterprise: An Economic History of New England* (Cambridge, MA: Harvard University Press, 2000); Lawrence W. Kennedy, *Planning the City Upon a Hill: Boston Since 1630* (Amherst: University of Massachusetts Press, 1992).

10. Cott, *Bonds of Womanhood*, 5–6, 20–36.

11. Cott, *Bonds of Womanhood*, 20.

12. Hamlin, "In Memoriam," 152.

13. Edward W. Tullidge, *The Women of Mormondom* (New York: Tullidge and Crandall, 1877), 441.

14. Jaques participated in the proxy baptism for her brother, who is listed as "Spencer Jaques," in 1841. Hamlin, "In Memoriam," 152; Susan Easton Black and Harvey Bischoff Black, eds., *Annotated Record of Baptisms for the Dead, 1840–1845: Nauvoo, Hancock County, Illinois*, 7 volumes (Provo, UT: Center for Family History and Genealogy, Brigham Young University, 2002), 5: 3260.

15. *The Boston Directory; Containing Names of the Inhabitants; Their Occupations, Places of Business and Dwelling Houses* (Boston: John H. A. Frost, 1827, and Charles Stimpson, Jr., 1829), 151, 154.

16. *The Boston Directory*, 151, 154.

17. Laurel Thatcher Ulrich, *A Midwife's Tale: The Life of Martha Ballard, Based on Her Diary, 1785–1812* (New York: Vintage Books, 1991), 33.

18. *The Boston Directory*, 151, 154.

NOTES

CHAPTER 2: SEEKING AND FINDING

1. "Methodist Churches in Boston Since 1792," Boston University, School of Theology Library, available at https://www.bu.edu/sthlibrary/archives/neccah/records-file-state/boston-records/.
2. George Hamlin, "In Memoriam," *Woman's Exponent* 12, no. 19 (1 March 1884): 152.
3. "The Testimony of Three Witnesses," Book of Mormon.
4. Some Boston area newspapers that Vienna may have had access to occasionally ran articles or stories about the Book of Mormon, Joseph Smith, and the new Latter-day faith. See, for example, "Golden Bible," *Salem Gazette*, 2 October 1829; "From the United States Gazette," *Salem Gazette*, 20 April 1830; "Lo! There," *Salem Gazette*, 10 December 1830; "Delusion," *Boston Courier*, 17 March 1831; "Fanaticism," *Christian Register* [Boston], 26 March 1831; "The Mormon Delusion," *Salem Gazette*, 6 May 1831. The source for Vienna's reading about the Church and Book of Mormon in a newspaper comes from "A Novel Excursion," *Deseret News*, 19 May 1875, 9.
5. Hamlin, "In Memoriam," 152.
6. Hamlin, "In Memoriam," 152.
7. Hamlin, "In Memoriam," 152.
8. Hamlin, "In Memoriam," 152.
9. *Boston Courier*, 10 October 1831, obtained from Ardis E. Parshall, "Vienna Jacques: A Glimpse in Transit," 10 April 2014, available from http://www.keepapitchinin.org/2014/04/10/vienna-jacques-a-glimpse-in-transit/, accessed 3 August 2015.
10. Revelation, 2 January 1831 [D&C 38], in *JSP*, D1: 232.
11. "Home Affairs," *Woman's Exponent* 7, no. 3 (1 July 1878): 21; Hamlin, "In Memoriam," 152; The Church of Jesus Christ of Latter-day Saints, Salt Lake City 12th Ward, Salt Lake City, Salt Lake Co., UT, Record of Members, [1849]–1941, 11, microfilm 26,723, U.S. and Canada Records Collection, FHL.
12. See Revelation, 20 July 1831 [D&C 57], and Revelation, 1 August 1831 [D&C 58], in *JSP*, D2: 5–21.
13. *Boston Courier*, 10 October 1831, obtained from Ardis E. Parshall. In her explanatory blog post, Parshall wrote, "The woman quoted in this story is unnamed, but the time, place, and circumstances identify her as Vienna Jacques, returning to Boston following her first visit to Kirtland. While intended to disparage Vienna, it nevertheless preserves the testimony borne to strangers by this remarkable early Latter-day Saint sister."
14. *Boston Courier*, 10 October 1831.
15. "Mormonites," *Eastern Argus* (Portland, Maine), 14 October 1831.
16. For more on the political ramifications of superstition, see Adam Jortner, "'Some Little Necromancy': Politics, Religion, and the Mormons, 1829–1838," in Spencer W. McBride, Brent M. Rogers, and Keith A. Erekson, eds., *Contingent Citizens: Shifting*

NOTES

Perceptions of Latter-day Saints in American Political Culture (Ithaca, NY: Cornell University Press, 2020), 17–28.
17. "Mormonites," *Eastern Argus*.

CHAPTER 3: A MISSIONARY

1. Christopher M.B. Allison, "Layered Lives: Boston Mormons and the Spatial Contexts of Conversion," *Journal of Mormon History* 42, no. 2 (April 2016): 174.
2. Samuel Harrison Smith, Diary, February 1832–May 1833, 22 June–7 August 1832, CHL; Orson Hyde, Journal, February–December 1832, 25 June–7 August 1832, CHL.
3. Revelation, 25 January 1832-A [D&C 75:1–22], in *JSP*, D2: 157–60.
4. "History of Orson Hyde," *The Latter-day Saints' Millennial Star* 26, no. 49 (3 December 1864): 775–76.
5. "History of Orson Hyde," *Millennial Star*, 775–76.
6. Laurel Thatcher Ulrich, *A House Full of Females: Plural Marriage and Women's Rights in Early Mormonism, 1835–1870* (New York: Alfred A. Knopf, 2017).
7. "Mormonism," *American Traveller* (Boston), 28 August 1832.
8. Wilford Woodruff, Journal, 11–14 May 1838, CHL.
9. Allison, "Layered Lives," 174.
10. "History of Orson Hyde," *Millennial Star*, 775–76.
11. Smith, Diary, 22 June–7 August 1832; Hyde, Journal, 25 June–7 August 1832.
12. Smith, Diary, 13 July 1832.
13. Smith, Diary, 13 July 1832.
14. See Smith, Diary, 22 June–7 August 1832; Hyde, Journal, 25 June–7 August 1832; and Hamlin, "In Memoriam," *Woman's Exponent* 12, no. 19 (1 March 1884): 152.
15. *Niles' Weekly Register* (Baltimore), 8 September 1832.
16. See Revelation, 20 July 1831 [D&C 57], in *JSP*, D2: 5–12; "The Elders in the Land of Zion to the Church of Christ Scattered Abroad," *The Evening and the Morning Star* 1, no. 2 (July 1832): 5; Scott H. Faulring, Kent P. Jackson, and Robert J. Matthews, eds., *Joseph Smith's New Translation of the Bible: Original Manuscripts* (Provo, UT: Religious Studies Center, Brigham Young University, 2004), 75–152.
17. "According to the common law," historian Laurel Thatcher Ulrich explains, "a woman's legal existence was 'suspended' in marriage. . . . Her earnings were her husband's to manage." (Laurel Thatcher Ulrich, "Runaway Wives, 1830–1860," *Journal of Mormon History* 42, no. 2 [April 2016]: 7.)
18. Smith, Diary, 22 July 1832.
19. Smith, Diary, 22 July 1832; Hyde, Journal, 21–22 July 1832.
20. Smith, Diary, 22 July 1832.
21. Smith, Diary, 22 July 1832.
22. George Hamlin later stated that Jaques had brought her sister into the Church,

NOTES

though Harriet is not stated by name. Hamlin provides no details about the sister's baptism. See Hamlin, "In Memoriam," 152.

23. Joseph Smith, letter to William W. Phelps, 27 November 1832, in *JSP*, D2: 321.
24. Similar situations must have happened in other cases over the next few years. For example, in 1835, Joseph Smith wrote about missionary work and of non-Mormon claims "that in preaching the doctrine of gathering, we break up families, and give license for men to leave their families; women their husbands; children their parents, and slaves their masters, thereby deranging the order, and breaking up the harmony and peace of society." These reports, Smith stated, were "detrimental to the cause of truth." He encouraged elders to preach to members of a family only with the permission of the head of the household so as to not engender conflict between husband and wife, parents and children, and society generally. ("To the elders of the church of Latter Day Saints," *Latter Day Saints' Messenger and Advocate* 1, no. 12 [September 1835]: 179–82; "To the elders of the church of the Latter Day Saints," *Latter Day Saints' Messenger and Advocate* 2, no. 2 [November 1835]: 209–212.)
25. See Ulrich, "Runaway Wives," 7.
26. Joseph Smith, letter to William W. Phelps, 27 November 1832, in *JSP*, D2: 321.

CHAPTER 4: A DONATION AND A REVELATION

1. George Hamlin, "In Memoriam," *Woman's Exponent* 12, no. 19 (1 March 1884): 152.
2. Joseph Smith III later claimed that one of his earliest memories in Kirtland was of Vienna Jaques in his family's home. He called Jaques "an eccentric woman and a 'young, old maid.'" Joseph Smith III was born on 6 November 1832, the same month that Vienna arrived in Kirtland. It is unlikely that Smith III had any memories of Jaques in Kirtland. (Joseph Smith III, *Memoirs of President Joseph Smith III* [Independence, MO: Price Publishing, 2001], 2; see also Fanny Stenhouse, *Tell it All: The Story of a Life's Experience in Mormonism* [Hartford, CT: A. D. Worthington, 1875], 253; Todd Compton, *In Sacred Loneliness: The Plural Wives of Joseph Smith* [Salt Lake City: Signature Books, 1997], 147.)
3. Joseph Smith, Junior, The Book of Mormon (Palmyra, NY: E. B. Grandin, 1830). This volume is found in the collection of the CHL, M222.1 B724 1830 no. 4.
4. Revelation, 27–28 December 1832 [D&C 88:119], in *JSP*, D2: 345.
5. Revelation, 2 January 1831 [D&C 38:32], in *JSP*, D1: 232.
6. Letter to William W. Phelps, 11 January 1833, in *JSP*, D2: 364–369.
7. Revelation, 8 March 1833 [D&C 90:30], in *JSP*, D3: 30–31.
8. See, for example, Susan Easton Black, "Happiness in Womanhood," *Ensign*, March 2002; Revelation, 8 March 1833 [D&C 90:28–29], in *JSP*, D3: 30–31.
9. Revelation, 8 March 1833 [D&C 90:28–29], in *JSP*, D3: 30–31; Edward W. Tullidge, *The Women of Mormondom* (New York: Tullidge and Crandall, 1877), 441; Hamlin, "In Memoriam," 152.

NOTES

10. This figure appears to have originated from Fawn Brodie's book *No Man Knows My History*. Brodie states that Jaques was a "bachelor woman with a modest capital of fourteen hundred dollars," and offers only Doctrine and Covenants section 90 as a source and no other primary documentation. (Fawn M. Brodie, *No Man Knows My History: The Life of Joseph Smith, Mormon Prophet* [New York: Alfred A. Knopf, 1990, second edition, first edition, 1945], 135.) No version of that revelation contains the $1,400 figure. I could not find any evidence of where Brodie obtained this figure while researching her papers housed at the University of Utah's Marriott Library. Others who mention Jaques and her donation use citations that can be traced back to Brodie or the nondescript citation to the revelation that she uses. Robert Kent Fielding's 1957 dissertation cites Brodie, "who places Miss Jacques contribution at $1400." (Robert Kent Fielding, "The Growth of the Mormon Church in Kirtland, Ohio," [PhD Diss., Indiana University, 1957], 72.) Lavina Fielding Anderson, who wrote that "a revelation received by Joseph Smith that same year directed her to consecrate her property—about $1400," also points to Brodie in her citation to this information. (Lavina Fielding Anderson, "Ministering Angels: Single Women in Mormon Society," *Dialogue* 16, no. 3 [Fall 1983]: 60.) Roger Launius's 1986 mention of Jaques's donation appears to cite to the RLDS version of the Doctrine and Covenants, section 87:7, much like Brodie simply cited to the LDS Doctrine and Covenants. (Roger D. Launius, *The Kirtland Temple: A Historical Narrative* [Independence, MO: Herald Publishing House, 1986], 38, 149.) Elwin C. Robison's work on the Kirtland Temple also mentions Jaques's $1,400 contribution, stating it was matched or exceeded only by Artemus Millett and John Tanner, but Robison only cites to Launius's aforementioned work. (Elwin C. Robison, *The First Mormon Temple: Design, Construction, and Historic Context of the Kirtland Temple* [Provo, UT: Brigham Young University Press, 1997], 99, 106.) Mark Staker cited to Robison when he mentioned Jaques's contribution to the Church. (Mark Lyman Staker, *Hearken, O Ye People: The Historical Setting of Joseph Smith's Ohio Revelations* [Salt Lake City: Greg Kofford Books, 2009], 436, 455.) Others have offered either no citation or a citation to the Doctrine and Covenants, like Brodie did. (See Black, "Happiness in Womanhood"; Susan Easton Black and Mary Jane Woodger, *Women of Character: Profiles of 100 Prominent LDS Women* [American Fork, UT: Covenant Communications, 2011], 144; Kristine Wardle Frederickson, *Extraordinary Courage: Women Empowered by the Gospel of Jesus Christ* [Salt Lake City: Eagle Gate, 2013], 12.)
11. "Mormonism," *American Traveller* (Boston), 28 August 1832.
12. Tullidge, *Women of Mormondom*, 441.
13. For more information on the land that the Church was purchasing see *JSP*, D3: 46–50, 108–12.
14. Joseph Smith, letter to Vienna Jaques, 4 September 1833, in *JSP*, D3: 292.
15. Maureen Ursenbach Beecher, ed., *The Personal Writings of Eliza Roxcy Snow* (Logan: Utah State University Press, 2000), 11.

NOTES

16. Beecher, *Personal Writings of Eliza Roxcy Snow*, 11; see also Janiece Johnson and Jennifer Reeder, *The Witness of Women: Firsthand Experiences and Testimonies from the Restoration* (Salt Lake City: Deseret Book, 2016), 119.
17. For more information on the involvement of women in the financial arena of the Church in the early 1830s, see Matthew C. Godfrey, "Wise Men and Wise Women: The Role of Church Members in Financing Church Operations, 1834–1835," *Journal of Mormon History* 43, no. 3 (2017): 1–21.

CHAPTER 5: ONWARD TO ZION

1. Revelation, 8 March 1833 [D&C 90:28–31], in *JSP*, D3: 24–32.
2. Revelation, 8 March 1833 [D&C 90:29, 31], in *JSP*, D3: 31.
3. Minutes, 30 April 1833, in *JSP*, D3: 71.
4. "Obituary," *The Evening and the Morning Star*, December 1833, vol. 2, 117.
5. Minutes, 30 April 1833, in *JSP*, D3: 71.
6. Sidney Rigdon, Joseph Smith, and Frederick G. Williams, Letter to Church Leaders in Jackson County, Missouri, 2 July 1833, in *JSP*, D3: 166.
7. Rigdon, Smith, and Williams, Letter to Church Leaders, in *JSP*, D3: 166; "Obituary," *Evening and Morning Star*, 117.
8. Rigdon, Smith, and Williams, Letter to Church Leaders, in *JSP*, D3: 166.
9. "The Elders Stationed in Zion to the Churches Abroad," *The Evening and the Morning Star*, July 1833, 110–111.
10. Revelation, 20 July 1831 [D&C 57], in *JSP*, D2: 5–12; Phelps, Biography, on JSP website.
11. Revelation, 1 November 1831–B [D&C 1], in Revelation Book 1, 125–27.
12. Letter from John Whitmer, 29 July 1833, in *JSP*, D3: 191, 193.
13. "Civil War in Missouri," *Cincinnati Journal*, 20 December 1833, 3.
14. Letter from John Whitmer, in *JSP*, D3: 191, 193; see also "To His Excellency, Daniel Dunklin," *The Evening and the Morning Star*, December 1833, 114–115; "Mormonism," *Kansas City [MO] Daily Journal*, 5 June 1881, 1.
15. Billy J. McMahon, "'Humane and Considerate Attention': Indian Removal from Missouri, 1803–1838," Master's thesis, Northwest Missouri State University, April 2013, 78–84.
16. John Corrill, *A Brief History of the Church of Christ of Latter Day Saints*, 1839, 19, in *JSP*, H2: 146.
17. "Mormonism," *Kansas City Daily Journal*, 1.
18. "Free People of Color," *The Evening and the Morning Star*, July 1833, 109.
19. Letter from John Whitmer, in *JSP*, D3: 192.
20. Letter from John Whitmer, in *JSP*, D3: 193.
21. "We the undersigned citizens of Jackson County," Edward Partridge Papers, CHL; "To His Excellency," *Evening and Morning Star*, 114; "'Regulating' the Mormonites," *Missouri Republican* (St. Louis), 9 August 1833, 3.

NOTES

22. Leonard J. Arrington and Susan Arrington Madsen, *Sunbonnet Sisters: True Stories of Mormon Women and Frontier Life* (Salt Lake City: Bookcraft, 1984), 16–17, 20; *Saints: The Story of The Church of Jesus Christ in the Latter Days, Volume 1: The Standard of Truth, 1815–1846* (Salt Lake City: The Church of Jesus Christ of Latter-day Saints, 2018), 177–179.
23. See, for example, Richard Lyman Bushman, *Joseph Smith: Rough Stone Rolling* (New York: Alfred A. Knopf, 2005), 178–180.
24. Manuscript History of the Church, vol. A-1, 327–28. See Letter from John Whitmer, in *JSP*, D3: 186–198.
25. Vienna Jaques, Statement, 22 February 1859, CHL; see also [Edward Partridge], "A History, of the Persecution," which appeared in the *Times and Seasons*, in December 1839, in *JSP*, H2: 209–211; see also Brady G. Winslow, "Vienna Jacques: Eyewitness to the Jackson County Persecutions," *Mormon Historical Studies* 11, no. 2 (Fall 2010): 93–98.
26. "Home Affairs," *Woman's Exponent* 7, no. 3 (1 July 1878): 21; George Hamlin, "In Memoriam," *Woman's Exponent* 12, no. 19 (1 March 1884): 152.
27. Vienna Jaques, Statement, 22 February 1859, CHL.
28. Manuscript History of the Church, vol. A-1, 327–28. See Letter from John Whitmer, in *JSP*, D3: 186–198.
29. Arrington and Madsen, *Sunbonnet Sisters*, 16–17, 20; *Saints, Volume 1*, 177–179.
30. "To His Excellency," *Evening and Morning Star*, 114; Corrill, *Brief History*, 19, in *JSP*, H2:146–147; John Whitmer, History, 42–44, in *JSP*, H2: 54–56; [Partridge], "A History, of the Persecution," in *JSP*, H2: 208–211.
31. "Memorandum of Agreement," 23 July 1833, CHL; "To His Excellency," *Evening and Morning Star*, 114–115.
32. Letter from John Whitmer, in *JSP*, D3: 190.

CHAPTER 6: A WORD OF COMFORT

1. Letter to Church Leaders in Jackson County, Missouri, 10 August 1833, in *JSP*, D3: 238; Letter to Church Leaders in Jackson County, Missouri, 18 August 1833, in *JSP*, D3: 259–269; Letter to Edward Partridge, 5 December 1833, in *JSP*, D3: 371–374; Letter to Edward Partridge and Others, 10 December 1833, in *JSP*, D3: 375–381.
2. Joseph Smith, letter to Vienna Jaques, 4 September 1833, in *JSP*, D3: 291–293.
3. Smith, letter to Vienna Jaques, in *JSP*, D3: 291–293.
4. Smith, letter to Vienna Jaques, in *JSP*, D3: 291–293; See Matthew 12:20 and Revelation, 6 June 1831 [D&C 52:11], in *JSP*, D1: 328.
5. Letter to Church Leaders, 10 August 1833, in *JSP*, D3: 243; Letter to Church Leaders, 18 August 1833, in *JSP*, D3: 262.
6. Smith, letter to Vienna Jaques, in *JSP*, D3: 291–293.
7. Smith, letter to Vienna Jaques, in *JSP*, D3: 291–293.

NOTES

8. Hyrum Smith, Diary, 7 June 1833, CHL; Ira Ames, Autobiography, 10, in Ira Ames, Autobiography and Journal, MS 6055, CHL; Frederick G. Williams, Kirtland, Ohio, to "Dear Brethren," 10 October 1833, in Joseph Smith, Letterbook 1, 57–58, CHL; Artemus Millet, Reminiscences, 3, MS 1600, CHL.
9. Smith, letter to Vienna Jaques, in *JSP*, D3: 291–293.
10. Smith, letter to Vienna Jaques, in *JSP*, D3: 291–293.
11. Letter to Church Leaders, 18 August 1833, in *JSP*, D3: 265.
12. Oliver Cowdery, Kirtland, Ohio, to John Whitmer, Missouri, 1 January 1834, in Cowdery, Letterbook, 14–17, CHL.
13. Rick Bennett, *Joseph T. Ball, Jr. (1804–1861)*, BlackPast.org, https://www.blackpast.org/african-american-history/ball-jr-joseph-t-1804-1861; Massachusetts Deaths, 1841–1915, Joseph T. Ball, 20 September 1861, Boston, Suffolk, Massachusetts, vol. /149, 132, State Archives, Boston, microfilm 960,179, U.S. and Canada Records Collection, FHL; Jeffrey D. Mahas, "Ball, Joseph T," Century of Black Mormons, available at https://exhibits.lib.utah.edu/s/century-of-black-mormons/page/ball-joseph-t.
14. Samuel Smith, Diary, 5 December 1832, CHL.
15. Smith, letter to Vienna Jaques, in *JSP*, D3: 291–293.
16. Smith, letter to Vienna Jaques, in *JSP*, D3: 291–293.
17. Samuel Smith, Diary, 26 June and 30 July 1832, CHL; Obituary for Mary Bailey Smith, *Times and Seasons*, 15 February 1841, 2: 324–225; Lucy Mack Smith, History, 1844–1845, bk. 14, 3, CHL.
18. Smith, letter to Vienna Jaques, in *JSP*, D3: 291–293.
19. Indicative of the egalitarian sentiment of Church members at this time, Smith had made earlier statements that he could write to anyone and that it was meant for all, though he infrequently corresponded with those in Missouri who were outside of the Church's leadership there. (Joseph Smith, letter to Edward Partridge, 2 May 1833, in *JSP*, D3: 75.)
20. "Home Affairs," *Woman's Exponent* 8, no. 2 (15 June 1879): 12.

CHAPTER 7: TRYING TIMES IN MISSOURI

1. See Memorandum of Agreement, 23 July 1833, CHL; see also Letter from John Whitmer, 29 July 1833, in *JSP*, D3: 186; [Edward Partridge], "A History, of the Persecution," *Times and Seasons*, December 1839, 1: 19, in *JSP*, H2: 211.
2. David Pettegrew, "A History of David Pettegrew," 17, in David Pettegrew Papers, 1840–1857, MS 2282, CHL.
3. Letter to Church Leaders in Jackson County, Missouri, 18 August 1833, in *JSP*, D3: 267.
4. Joseph Smith History, vol. A-1, JSP, https://www.josephsmithpapers.org/paper-summary/history-1838-1856-volume-a-1-23-december-1805-30-august-1834/43, 346,; John Corrill, *A Brief History of the Church of Christ of Latter Day Saints*, 1839,

NOTES

19, in *JSP*, H2: 147; see also "To His Excellency, Daniel Dunklin," *The Evening and the Morning Star*, December 1833, 114–115.
5. Letter to Church Leaders, 18 August 1833, in *JSP*, D3: 264–65, 269.
6. Revised Plat of the City of Zion, circa early August 1833, in *JSP*, D3: 244–258.
7. See Historical Introduction to Letter, 30 October 1833, in *JSP*, D3: 332–333; see also "From Missouri," *The Evening and the Morning Star*, January 1834, 124–126; Corrill, *Brief History*, in *JSP*, H2: 147.
8. Letter, 30 October 1833, in *JSP*, D3: 335; "The Outrage in Jackson County, Missouri," *The Evening and the Morning Star*, December 1833, 118.
9. Letter, 30 October 1833, in *JSP*, D3: 335.
10. [Partridge], "A History, of the Persecution," in *JSP*, H2:213.
11. "The Outrage in Jackson County," *Evening and Morning Star*, 118; Corrill, *Brief History*, 19–20, in *JSP*, H2: 147–148.
12. "From Missouri," *Evening and Morning Star*, 125; [Partridge], "A History, of the Persecution," in *JSP*, H2: 218.
13. [Partridge], "A History, of the Persecution," in *JSP*, H2: 219–220. Pitcher apparently told Church members he would return their arms as soon as they left the county, though he never did. (Corrill, *Brief History*, 44, in *JSP*, H2: 191; see also H2: 63n193, 73n220.)
14. Parley P. Pratt, *History of the Late Persecution Inflicted by the State of Missouri upon the Mormons* (Detroit: Dawson and Bates, 1839), 22, CHL; Letter from William W. Phelps, 6–7 November 1833, in *JSP*, D3: 341.
15. Isaac McCoy, "The Disturbances in Jackson County," *Missouri Republican* [St. Louis], 20 December 1833, 2–3; Pratt, *History of the Late Persecution*, 21; see also [Partridge], "A History, of the Persecution," in *JSP*, H2: 221–222.
16. [Partridge], "A History, of the Persecution," in *JSP*, H2: 222; John Whitmer, History, 45, in *JSP*, H2: 57.
17. See Letter from Edward Partridge, between 14 and 19 November 1833, in *JSP*, D3: 344–350; Letter from William W. Phelps, 14 November 1833, in *JSP*, D3: 342–43; and Letter from John Corrill, 17 November 1833, in *JSP*, D3: 351–354.
18. Emily M. Austin, *Mormonism; or, Life among the Mormons: Being an Autobiographical Sketch; Including an Experience of Fourteen Years of Mormon Life* (Madison, Wisconsin: M.J. Cantwell, 1882), 72–73.
19. Revelation, 12 October 1833 [D&C 100:13], in *JSP*, D3: 325.
20. Letter to the Church in Clay County, MO, 22 January 1834, in *JSP*, D3: 408–412. Daniel Dunklin, Jefferson City, MO, to William W. Phelps et al., 4 February 1834; Edward Partridge et al., Petition to Andrew Jackson, 10 April 1834; William W. Phelps, Liberty, MO, to Thomas H. Benton, 10 April 1834; Lewis Cass, Washington DC, to Sidney Gilbert et al., Liberty, MO, 2 May 1834. These letters are found in William W. Phelps, Collection of Missouri Documents, CHL.

NOTES

21. Revelation, 24 February 1834 [D&C 103:12–13, 21–22, 30, 37–40], in *JSP*, D3: 460–462.
22. For more information on the Camp of Israel, also known as Zion's Camp, see, for example, Matthew C. Godfrey, "'The Redemption of Zion Must Needs Come by Power': Insights into the Camp of Israel Expedition, 1834," *BYU Studies Quarterly* 53, no. 4 (2014): 125–146; Andrea G. Radke, "We Also Marched: The Women and Children of Zion's Camp, 1834," *BYU Studies* 39, no. 1 (2000): 147–165; Bruce A. Van Orden, "Zion's Camp: A Refiner's Fire," in Larry C. Porter and Susan Easton Black, eds., *The Prophet Joseph: Essays on the Life and Mission of Joseph Smith* (Salt Lake City: Deseret Book, 1988), 192–207; Warren A. Jennings, "The Army of Israel Marches into Missouri," *Missouri Historical Review* 62, no. 2 (January 1968): 107–135.
23. Joseph B. Noble, Journal, 8-9, in Joseph B. Noble reminiscences, ca. 1836, MS 1031, CHL.
24. Heber C. Kimball, "Extracts from H. C. Kimball's Journal," *Times and Seasons* 6, no. 5 (15 March 1845): 839–40.
25. Minutes and Prayer of Dedication, 27 March 1836, in *JSP*, D5: 188–209.
26. Joseph Smith, Journal, 3 April 1836, in *JSP*, J1: 219–222; Visions, 3 April 1836, in *JSP*, D5: 224–229.
27. Malachi 4:5–6; 3 Nephi 25:5–6.
28. Edward Partridge, Journal, ca. May 1836, CHL; Historical Introduction to Application for Land Patent, 22 June 1836, in *JSP*, D5: 253–256.
29. Letter from William W. Phelps, 7 July 1837, in *JSP*, D5: 402.
30. Doctrine and Covenants 115:6–8.
31. See Minutes, 12 and 13 April 1838, in *JSP*, D6: 83–103.
32. Woodruff, Journal, 9 May 1838, CHL.

CHAPTER 8: REDRESS

1. Lucy Walker Kimball, quoted in Lyman Omer Littlefield, *Reminiscences of Latter-day Saints* (Logan, UT: The Utah Journal Co., 1888), 39–40.
2. See John Corrill, *A Brief History of the Church of Christ of Latter Day Saints*, 1839, 19, in *JSP*, H2: 146; also in Karen Lynn Davidson, Richard L. Jensen, and David J. Whitaker, eds., *Histories 2, Assigned Histories, 1831–1847*, *JSP*, H2: 183, 186.
3. Isaac Leany petition in Clark V. Johnson, ed., *Mormon Redress Petitions: Documents of the 1833–1838 Missouri Conflict* (Provo, UT: Religious Studies Center, Brigham Young University, 1992), 268.
4. Brent M. Rogers, "To the 'Honest and Patriotic Sons of Liberty': Mormon Appeals for Redress and Social Justice, 1843–44," *Journal of Mormon History* 39, no. 1 (Winter 2013): 58–60.
5. David Lewis, quoted in "A History of the Persecution, of the Church of Jesus Christ

NOTES

of Latter-day Saints in Missouri," in *Times and Seasons* 1, no. 10 (August 1840): 149–50; also, in *JSP*, H2: 269.

6. William G. Hartley, "'Almost Too Intolerable a Burthen:' The Winter Exodus from Missouri, 1838–39," *Journal of Mormon History* 18 (Fall 1992): 24; Edward W. Tullidge, *The Women of Mormondom* (New York: Tullidge and Crandall, 1877), 174.

7. Joseph Holbrook, "The Life of Joseph Holbrook, 1806–1871," typescript, 46, L. Tom Perry Special Collections, Harold B. Lee Library, Brigham Young University, Provo, Utah.

8. Amanda Smith, quoted in Emmeline B. Wells, "Amanda Smith," *Woman's Exponent* 9, no. 24 (15 May 1881): 189.

9. "Letter to the Editor," *Missouri Republican*, 7 December 1838, 2.

10. John Hammer, quoted in Littlefield, *Reminiscences of Latter-day Saints*, 72–73.

11. "Editorial," *Quincy Whig*, 2 March 1839, 2; "The Mormons," *Quincy Whig*, 16 March 1839, 1.

12. Woodruff, Journal, 17–18 March 1839, CHL.

13. Joseph Smith and others to Church Members and Edward Partridge, 20 March 1839, manuscript, pt. 2, 5, [D&C 123:1], JSP, Revelations Collection, CHL.

14. Johnson, *Mormon Redress Petitions*, xxv, xxvii.

15. Far West and Nauvoo Elders' Certificates, 1837–46, CHL; D. Michael Quinn, *The Mormon Hierarchy: Origins of Power* (Salt Lake City: Signature Books, 1994), 484; Far West Committee Minutes, January–April 1839, CHL; International Society Daughters of Utah Pioneers, *Pioneer Women of Faith and Fortitude* 4 vols. (Salt Lake City: Publishers Press, 1998), 4: 2740.

16. For more on female legal identity in the United States at this time, see Marylynn Salmon, *Women and the Law of Property in Early America* (Chapel Hill: University of North Carolina Press, 1986), 14–18; Linda K. Kerber, "A Constitutional Right to be Treated like American Ladies: Women and the Obligations of Citizenship," in Linda K. Kerber, Alice Kessler-Harris, and Kathryn Kish Sklar, eds., *U. S. History as Women's History: New Feminist Essays* (Chapel Hill: University of North Carolina Press, 1995), 20–22; Laurel Thatcher Ulrich, *The Age of Homespun: Objects and Stories in the Creation of an American Myth* (New York: Alfred A. Knopf, 2001), 110–11, 137; Daniel Shearer, Affidavit, 7 May 1839, in Johnson, *Mormon Redress Petitions*, 336–337.

17. Shearer, Affidavit, in Johnson, ed., *Mormon Redress Petitions*, 336–337.

18. Shearer, Affidavit, in Johnson, ed., *Mormon Redress Petitions*, 336–337.

19. Eliza R. Snow, "The Slaughter on Shoal Creek, Caldwell County, Missouri," *Times and Seasons* 1, no. 2 (December 1839): 32.

20. "Horrors of the Missouri Democracy," *New York Spectator*, 1 July 1839, 4.

21. "Great Meeting in Behalf of Mormon Women and Children," *New York Morning Herald*, 17 September 1839.

22. *Deseret News*, 24 April 1854.

NOTES

23. James Adams to Martin Van Buren, 9 November 1839, Van Buren Correspondence, CHL.
24. Joseph Smith and Elias Higbee to Hyrum Smith and the High Council, 5 December 1839, Letterbook 2: 85, MS 155, box 2, folder 2, CHL.
25. Joseph Smith, Sidney Rigdon, and Elias Higbee, 27 January 1840, Records of the United States Senate, 26th–28th Congress, RG 46, bx 91, National Archives, Washington, DC.
26. Senate Report, 4 March 1840, 26th Congress, 1st Session, Congressional Globe.
27. Shearer appears to have spent much time away from Nauvoo in the early 1840s, including serving a mission to New York to electioneer for Joseph Smith's presidential campaign in 1844. (Untitled article, *Times and Seasons* 1, no. 4 [February 1840]: 61; "Special Conference," *Times and Seasons* 5, no. 8 [15 April 1844]: 505.) On 3 February 1846, Daniel Shearer was endowed at the Nauvoo Temple and was assigned to the Sixth Wagon Company in the evacuation of Nauvoo, a different one from Jaques who received the temple ritual Latter-day Saints called the "endowment" in January 1846. Couples and families were typically assigned together. That they were endowed at different times and assigned different companies indicates that Jaques and Shearer were separated by early 1846. Shearer eventually made his way to Salt Lake City in October 1852 and lived in the city's 13th Ward. (Sherwin Chase, "Information Concerning Daniel Shearer, circa 1983," CHL.)

CHAPTER 9: A WITNESS

1. Discourse, ca. 19 July 1840, in *JSP*, D7: 341–342.
2. *JSP*, D7: xxiii.
3. Ordinance work for the dead, which became possible with the bestowal of priesthood keys upon Joseph Smith in the Kirtland Temple on 3 April 1836, would emerge as one of the most fundamentally distinctive Latter-day Saint doctrines (see Joseph Smith, Journal, 3 April 1836, in *JSP*, J1: 219).
4. "Brunson, Seymour," Biography, Joseph Smith Papers, available at https://www.josephsmithpapers.org/person/seymour-brunson.
5. Obituary for Seymour Brunson, *Times and Seasons* 1, (September 1840): 176.
6. Jane Harper Neyman Fisher, Biography, in Jill Mulvay Derr, Carol Cornwall Madsen, Kate Holbrook, and Matthew J. Grow, eds. *The First Fifty Years of Relief Society: Key Documents in Latter-Day Saint Women's History* (Salt Lake City: Church Historian's Press, 2016).
7. Jane H. Neyman, "Be Forbearing and Forgiving," 4 November 1869, Historical Intro., in Jennifer Reeder and Kate Holbrook, eds. *At the Pulpit: 185 Years of Discourses by Latter-day Saint Women* (Salt Lake City: Church Historian's Press, 2017), chapter 12.
8. Alexander L. Baugh, "'For This Ordinance Belongeth to My House': The Practice of

NOTES

Baptism for the Dead Outside the Nauvoo Temple," *Mormon Historical Studies* 3, no. 1 (Spring 2002): 47–48.

9. Address, 1839–1842, in the Joseph Smith Collection, MS 155, CHL; Statements in regard to Baptism for the Dead, Nauvoo, "Joseph Smith History Documents, 1839–1860," 13 September 1840, CHL; Joseph Smith, Sermon, 15 August 1840, Reminiscent account of Simon Baker, Journal History, 15 August 1840, CHL.
10. Vilate Kimball, letter to Heber C. Kimball, 11 October 1840, "Vilate M. Kimball Letters, 1840," CHL.
11. Statements in regard to Baptism for the Dead, Vienna Jaques, 29 November 1854, CHL.
12. Address, 1839–1842, in the Joseph Smith Collection, CHL; Statements in regard to Baptism for the Dead, 13 September 1840, CHL.
13. Jaques gave her statement on that event to the Historian's Office on 29 November 1854, in Salt Lake City, Utah. See Statements in regard to Baptism for the Dead, 13 September 1840, CHL; Ryan C. Tobler, "'Saviors on Mount Zion': Mormon Sacramentalism, Mortality, and the Baptism for the Dead," *Journal of Mormon History* 39 (2013): 182–238; Laurel Thatcher Ulrich, *A House Full of Females: Plural Marriage and Women's Rights in Early Mormonism, 1835–1870* (New York: Alfred A. Knopf, 2017), 293.
14. Kimball, letter to Heber C. Kimball, 11 October 1840, CHL.
15. Phebe Carter Woodruff, Letter to Wilford Woodruff, 6–19 October 1840, Wilford Woodruff, Collection, CHL.
16. Joseph Smith, Sermon, 4 October 1840, in "Minutes of the general conference of the church of Jesus Christ of Latter Day Saints, held in Nauvoo, Hancock county, Ill. Oct., 3rd 1840," *Times and Seasons* 1, no. 12 (October 1840): 186.
17. Kimball, letter to Heber C. Kimball, 11 October 1840, CHL.
18. Kimball, letter to Heber C. Kimball, 11 October 1840, CHL.
19. Vienna Jaques, letter to Brigham Young, 2 July 1870, Incoming Correspondence, Brigham Young Collection, CHL. For more information on baptisms for the dead in Nauvoo, see Baugh, "'For This Ordinance Belongeth to My House,'" 47–58.
20. Susan Easton Black and Harvey Bischoff Black, eds., *Annotated Record of Baptisms for the Dead, 1840–1845: Nauvoo, Hancock County, Illinois*, 7 volumes (Provo, UT: Center for Family History and Genealogy, Brigham Young University, 2002), 5:3256–3265.
21. Letter to Quorum of the Twelve, 15 December 1840, in *JSP*, D7: 470.
22. "Baptism for the Dead," *New York Tribune*, 4 August 1841; *JSP*, D8: xxxi.
23. "Mormon Interpretation of 1 Cor. 15:29," *Ohio Observer*, 26 August 1841.
24. M. Guy Bishop, "'What Has Become of Our Fathers?': Baptism for the Dead at Nauvoo," *Dialogue: A Journal of Mormon Thought* 23, no. 2 (Summer 1990): 88–89.
25. Discourse, 7 April 1844, *Times and Seasons*, 15 August 1844, 616.
26. Doctrine and Covenants 128:15.

NOTES

CHAPTER 10: THE TEMPLE

1. For teachings on the building of the temple see Discourse, ca. 19 July 1840, in *JSP*, D7: 344; Minutes and Discourse, 3–5 October 1840, in *JSP*, D7: 422.
2. Revelation, 19 January 1841 [D&C 124], in *JSP*, D7: 517.
3. Minutes and Discourse, 1–5 October 1841, in *JSP*, D8: 289–290.
4. Thomas Wentworth Storrow, "Journey to the West," Storrow Family Papers, 1762–1999, Massachusetts Historical Society, 3 July 1841; Richard Lyman Bushman, *Joseph Smith: Rough Stone Rolling* (New York: Alfred A. Knopf, 2005), 424–425.
5. Susan Easton Black and Harvey Bischoff Black, eds., *Annotated Record of Baptisms for the Dead, 1840–1845: Nauvoo, Hancock County, Illinois*, 7 volumes (Provo, UT: Center for Family History and Genealogy, Brigham Young University, 2002), 5:3256–3265.
6. Discourse, ca. 19 July 1840, in *JSP*, D7: 344.
7. Minutes and Discourse, 3–5 October 1840, in *JSP*, D7: 423.
8. Letter to Quorum of the Twelve, 15 December 1840, in *JSP*, D7: 466.
9. *JSP*, J2: 280–285.
10. Margaret Kennedy, Church History Biographical Database, CHL.
11. *JSP*, J2: 280–285; Steven C. Dinger, "'The Doctors in This Region Don't Know Much': Medicine and Obstetrics in Mormon Nauvoo," *Journal of Mormon History* 42, no. 4 (October 2016): 51–68.
12. Wilford Woodruff, Journal, 11 June 1843, CHL.
13. Revelation, 19 January 1841 [D&C 124:28], in *JSP*, D7: 517.
14. Joseph Smith, Journal, 4 May 1842, in *JSP*, J2: 53; see also Ronald K. Esplin, Dean C. Jessee, Brent M. Rogers, Gerrit J. Dirkmaat, and Andrew H. Hedges, eds., *The Brigham Young Journals*, vol. 1 (Provo, UT: Brigham Young University Press, 2023), Editorial Note, 127–128.
15. *JSP*, J3: xxi; Joseph Smith, Journal, 29 May 1843, in *JSP*, J3: 25.
16. Instruction, 2 April 1843, in *JSP*, D12: 139.
17. "Remarks," *Times and Seasons*, 6 (1 January 1846): 1084.
18. Jacob Scott to Mary Scott Warnock, 5 January 1844, Community of Christ Library and Archives.
19. Discourse, 16 July 1843, in *JSP*, D12: 487.
20. Helen Mar Kimball Whitney, Autobiography, 1–2, CHL.
21. Dan Jones, "The Martyrdom of Joseph Smith and His Brother Hyrum," introduced by Ronald D. Dennis, in *BYU Studies Quarterly* 24, no. 1 (1984): 92–93.
22. Zina Huntington Jacobs, Diary, 28 and 30 June 1844, CHL.
23. Jones, "The Martyrdom of Joseph Smith and His Brother Hyrum," 93, 108–109.
24. "Events of the Week," *Warsaw Signal*, 29 June 1844, 2.
25. Brigham Young, Journal, 12–17 January 1846, in BY J1: 299–302.
26. Brigham Young, Journal, 19–23 January 1846, in BY J1: 304–305.
27. Temple Records Index Bureau, *Nauvoo Temple Endowment Register: 10 December*

NOTES

1845 to 8 February 1846 (Salt Lake City: The Church of Jesus Christ of Latter-day Saints, 1974), 179, 285.
28. Sarah DeArmon Pea Rich, 1814–1893, Autobiography, typescript, BYU.
29. Sherwin Chase, "Information Concerning Daniel Shearer, circa 1983," CHL.

CHAPTER 11: ONWARD TO THE ROCKY MOUNTAINS

1. Kenneth W. Godfrey, Audrey M. Godfrey, and Jill Mulvay Derr, *Women's Voices: An Untold History of the Latter-day Saints, 1830–1900* (Salt Lake City, UT: Deseret Book Company, 1982), 156.
2. Godfrey, Godfrey, and Derr, *Women's Voices*, 190, 195.
3. See Maurine Carr Ward, ed., *Winter Quarters: The 1846–1848 Life Writings of Mary Haskin Parker Richards* (Logan, UT: Utah State University Press, 1996).
4. Richard E. Bennett, *Mormons at the Missouri: Winter Quarters, 1846–1852* (Norman, OK: University of Oklahoma Press, 2004), 134.
5. Newel Knight, Journal, 17 November 1846, CHL.
6. Ursalia B. Hastings Hascall to Col. Wilson Andrews, 19 September 1846, in *The Nauvoo Journal* 5, no. 1 (Spring 1993): 13.
7. Brigham Young to Charles C. Rich, 4 January 1847, CR 1234 1, box 16, folder 11, CHL.
8. Nathan T. Porter, Reminiscences, ca. 1879, CHL.
9. Daniel Shearer, Church History Biographical Database, CHL.
10. Sarah DeArmon Pea Rich, Autobiography, 1885–1893, [manuscript:] folder 2, 27–43, CHL.
11. Mary Ann Phelps Rich, Autobiography, 19–21, CHL.
12. Porter, Reminiscences, ca. 1879, CHL.
13. Sarah DeArmon Pea Rich, Autobiography, folder 2, 27–43, CHL.
14. Charles C. Rich, Journal, 17 July 1847, CHL.
15. Sarah DeArmon Pea Rich, Autobiography, folder 2, 27–43, CHL.
16. Sarah DeArmon Pea Rich, Autobiography, folder 2, 27–43, CHL.
17. Mary Ann Phelps Rich, Autobiography, 19–21, CHL.
18. "Past Celebrations of Pioneer Day," *Salt Lake Herald*, 15 April 1897, 8.
19. Charles C. Rich, Journal, 23–24 July 1847, CHL.
20. Charles C. Rich, Journal, 1 August 1847, CHL.
21. Porter, Reminiscences, ca. 1879, CHL.
22. Emeline Grover Rich, Autobiography and Diary 1890–1909, 25–29, CHL.
23. Mary Ann Phelps Rich, Autobiography, 19–21, CHL.
24. Charles C. Rich, Journal, 24 June and 30 July 1847, CHL; Emeline Grover Rich, Autobiography and Diary, 29, CHL.
25. Historical Department, Journal History of the Church, 21 June 1847, CHL. For more on the Charles C. Rich Company and its movement, see Charles C. Rich, 1846–1847 Diary, CHL; and Leonard J. Arrington, *Charles C. Rich* (Provo, UT:

NOTES

Brigham Young University Press, 1974), 111–123. Arrington does not list Jaques as among the people in Rich's company. For more information on those early Church members who traveled to Utah, see The Church of Jesus Christ of Latter-day Saints, Church History Department's website, the Church History Biographical database, available at https://history.churchofjesuschrist.org/chd/landing.

CHAPTER 12: A LITTLE MILK

1. Revelation, 8 March 1833, in *JSP*, D3: 31.
2. Vienna Jaques, Letter to Brigham Young, 16 October 1848, CHL.
3. Jaques, Letter to Brigham Young, 16 October 1848, CHL.
4. Harriet W. Young, Journal, 27 May 1848, in Lorenzo D. Young Papers, MS 1538, CHL.
5. John G. Turner, *Brigham Young: Pioneer Prophet* (Cambridge, MA: The Belknap Press of Harvard University Press, 2012), 179.
6. Agreement, Vienna Jaques and Joseph F. Smith, 31 December 1881, Joseph F. Smith Papers, CHL.
7. Claire Noall, letter to Fawn Brodie, 16 September 1943, Matthew Frederick and Claire Wilcox Noall Papers, J. Willard Marriott Library, Special Collections, University of Utah (hereafter MLSC).
8. Daniel A. Sanborn, "Salt Lake City, 1889: Sheet 034," Sanborn Map Collection, MLSC, available at https://collections.lib.utah.edu/ark:/87278/s6dn4g8p.
9. Quoted in Laurie J. Bryant, *A Modest Homestead: Life in Small Adobe Homes in Salt Lake City, 1850–1897* (Salt Lake City: University of Utah Press, 2017), 17.
10. Bryant, *A Modest Homestead*, 17.
11. Andrew Jenson, *Latter-day Saint Biographical Encyclopedia*, Vol. 1. (Salt Lake City: Andrew Jenson History Company and Deseret News Press, 1901), 236–237.
12. Daughters of Utah Pioneers, *Pioneer Women of Faith and Fortitude*, (Salt Lake City: International Daughters of Utah Pioneers and Publishers Press, 1998), 4:2740.
13. Bryant, *A Modest Homestead*, 3–9.
14. Sanborn, "Salt Lake City, 1889: Sheet 034."
15. 1850 Utah Territorial Census, Salt Lake County, 51, CHL; Noall, letter to Fawn Brodie, 16 September 1943, MLSC; George Hamlin, "In Memoriam," *Woman's Exponent* 12, no. 19 (1 March 1884): 152.
16. Mrs. B. G. Ferris, *The Mormons at Home; With some Incidents of Travel from Missouri to California, 1852–3* (New York: Dix & Edwards, 1856), 124.
17. Jill Mulvay Derr, Carol Cornwall Madsen, Kate Holbrook, and Matthew J. Grow, eds. *The First Fifty Years of Relief Society: Key Documents in Latter-Day Saint Women's History* (Salt Lake City: Church Historian's Press, 2016), Part 2 Introduction, 179; Female Council of Health, MS 3195, CHL.
18. See Patty Sessions, Diary, 9–11 February 1853, see also 27 February 1853, CHL; Wilford Woodruff, Journal, 11 February 1853, CHL.

NOTES

19. Noall, letter to Fawn Brodie, 16 September 1943, MLSC.
20. Jennifer J. Hill, *Birthing the West: Mothers and Midwives in the Rockies and Plains* (Lincoln: University of Nebraska Press, 2022), 60.
21. Hill, *Birthing the West*, 10.
22. Ferris, *The Mormons at Home*, 199.
23. Ferris, *The Mormons at Home*, 199, 200; Ulrich, *House Full of Females*, 293.
24. Ferris, *The Mormons at Home*, 200.
25. Ferris, *The Mormons at Home*, 204.
26. Ferris, *The Mormons at Home*, 124.
27. Ferris, *The Mormons at Home*, 125.
28. Ferris, The Mormons at Home, 154–156.
29. Derr, et. al., *First Fifty Years of Relief Society*, 181–182.
30. Historical Department, Journal History of the Church, 29 November 1854, CHL.
31. Dan Vogel, ed., *History of Joseph Smith and The Church of Jesus Christ of Latter-day Saints: A Source and Text-Critical Edition, Volume 1: 1805–1833* (Salt Lake City: The Smith-Petit Foundation, 2015), xcv.
32. For more information on the Word of Wisdom, see *JSP*, D3: 11–24; Paul H. Peterson, "An Historical Analysis of the Word of Wisdom," Master's thesis, Brigham Young University, 1972; and Paul H. Peterson and Ronald W. Walker, "Brigham Young's Word of Wisdom Legacy," *BYU Studies* 42, nos. 3 & 4 (2003): 29–64.
33. Vienna Jaques, letter to Brigham Young, 11 September 1855, Brigham Young Collection, Incoming Correspondence, CHL.
34. In a September 1859 letter, Jaques wrote that Young had "always answered" the call of her previous letters. Jaques, letter to Brigham Young, 13 September 1859, CHL. In another letter Jaques again noted Young's willingness to always consider her letters. Jaques, letter to Brigham Young, 2 July 1870, CHL.
35. "Home Affairs," *Woman's Exponent* 7, no. 3 (1 July 1878): 21. Two sources indicate that she took care of elderly men in need later in her life. In a letter to Brigham Young in September 1859, Jaques stated that an "old man Tattersall" lived with her and that she tried "to take good care of him." (Jaques, letter to Brigham Young, 13 September 1859, CHL.) In addition, the 1880 Utah Territorial census lists a seventy-six-year old named Philip Huett as residing with Jaques, who was listed as the head of household. (1880 Census, Utah Territory, Salt Lake County, 8, CHL.)
36. Noall, letter to Fawn Brodie, 16 September 1943, MLSC.
37. "List of Prizes," *Deseret News*, 21 October 1857. Jaques was apparently not a member of the society and could not be awarded the money associated with the prize. The Deseret Agricultural and Manufacturing Society was created by the Utah territorial legislature in 1856, but with the arrival of the U.S. Army and the Utah War of 1857–58, its activities were minimized. (Leonard J. Arrington, *Great Basin Kingdom: An Economic History of the Latter-day Saints, 1830–1900* [Salt Lake City: University of Utah Press, 1993, reprint], 226.)

NOTES

CHAPTER 13: A SEALING

1. Mrs. B. G. Ferris, *The Mormons at Home; With some Incidents of Travel from Missouri to California, 1852–3* (New York: Dix & Edwards, 1856), 126.
2. Daniel Shearer, Church History Biographical Database, CHL; Sherwin Chase, "Information Concerning Daniel Shearer, circa 1983," CHL.
3. Historical Introduction, Revelation, 21 July 1843, in JSP, D12: 459; see also D&C 132:19–20.
4. Temple Records Index Cards, Reed C. Durham Papers, MLSC; Helen Mar Kimball Whitney, Autobiography, 1–2, CHL.
5. Ferris, *The Mormons at Home*, 126.
6. Laurel Thatcher Ulrich, *A House Full of Females: Plural Marriage and Women's Rights in Early Mormonism, 1835–1870* (New York: Alfred A. Knopf, 2017), 293.
7. Ulrich, *House Full of Females*, 231.
8. Solomon Nunes Carvalho, *Incidents of Travel and Adventure in the Far West with Colonel Fremont's Last Expedition* (Lincoln: University of Nebraska Press, 2004), 178–179.
9. Ferris, *The Mormons at Home*, 126.
10. Ferris, *The Mormons at Home*, 126.
11. Ferris, *The Mormons at Home*, 126.
12. Cited in Todd Compton, "A Trajectory of Plurality: An Overview of Joseph Smith's Thirty-three Plural Wives," *Dialogue: A Journal of Mormon Thought* 29, no. 2 (Summer 1996): 4, 36. Lavina Fielding Anderson accepts the unsigned affidavit as proof that Joseph Smith and Jaques wed in "about 1843 or 1844." (Lavina Fielding Anderson, "Ministering Angels: Single Women in Mormon Society," *Dialogue* 16, no. 3 [Fall 1983]: 60.)
13. Nancy Alexander, Statement, Typescript in Stanley B. Kimball Papers, Southern Illinois University; photocopy in Linda King Newell Collection, MLSC; Brian C. Hales and Gregory L. Smith, "A Response to Grant Palmer's 'Sexual Allegations against Joseph Smith and the Beginnings of Polygamy in Nauvoo,'" *Interpreter: A Journal of Mormon Scripture* 12 (2014): 183–236; see also Brian C. Hales, "Fanny Alger and Joseph Smith's Pre-Nauvoo Reputation," *Journal of Mormon History* 35, no. 4 (Fall 2009): 112–190.
14. Claire Noall, letter to Fawn Brodie, 16 September 1943, Matthew Frederick and Claire Wilcox Noall Papers, MLSC; Vesta P. Crawford Papers, MLSC.
15. Fawn Brodie, letter to Claire Noall, 22 June 1944, Noall Papers, MLSC; Fawn McKay Brodie Papers, MLSC.
16. Fawn M. Brodie, *No Man Knows My History: The Life of Joseph Smith, Mormon Prophet* (New York: Alfred A. Knopf, 1990, second edition), 486; see also Todd Compton, "Fawn Brodie on Joseph Smith's Plural Wives and Polygamy: A Critical View," in Newell G. Bringhurst, ed. *Reconsidering No Man Knows My History: Fawn*

NOTES

Brodie and Joseph Smith in Retrospect (Logan: Utah State University Press, 1996), 183.
17. "The Memoirs of President Joseph Smith, edited by his daughter Mary Audentia Smith Anderson," in *The Saints' Herald* 82 (October 1935): 1328–29.
18. Todd Compton, *In Sacred Loneliness: The Plural Wives of Joseph Smith* (Salt Lake City: Signature Books, 1997), 2, 8–9.

CHAPTER 14: A LITTLE TROUBLE

1. For more on these events see Brent M. Rogers, *Unpopular Sovereignty: Mormons and the Federal Management of Early Utah Territory* (Lincoln: University of Nebraska Press, 2017); Ronald W. Walker, Richard E. Turley Jr., and Glen M. Leonard, *Massacre at Mountain Meadows* (New York: Oxford University Press, 2008); Richard D. Poll, "The Move South," *BYU Studies* 29, no. 4 (1989): 65–88.
2. Historical Department, Journal History of the Church, 22 February 1859, 1, CR 100 137, CHL.
3. "History of Joseph Smith," *Millennial Star* 14 (25 September 1852), 486.
4. Journal History, 22 February 1859, CHL.
5. Epistle to the Saints, 16 November 1845, Willard Richards, Journals and Papers, 1821–1854, CHL; Robin Scott Jensen, "'Archives of the Better World': The Nineteenth-Century Historian's Office and Mormonism's Archival Flexibility," PhD Diss., University of Utah, 2019, 76.
6. Jensen, "'Archives of the Better World,'" 76.
7. Journal History, 4 March 1859, CHL.
8. Journal History, 4 March 1859, CHL; Letter to Vienna Jaques, in *JSP*, D3: 296.
9. Journal History, 4 March 1859, CHL; Letter to Vienna Jaques, in *JSP*, D3: 296.
10. Edward W. Tullidge, *History of Salt Lake City* (Salt Lake City: Star Printing Company, 1886), 171.
11. Vienna Jaques, letter to Brigham Young, 13 September 1859, CHL.
12. Jaques, letter to Young, 13 September 1859, CHL.
13. Brigham Young to Vienna Jaques, 7 November 1859, in Brigham Young, Letterbook 5, 304, CR 1234 1, CHL.
14. Young to Jaques, 7 November 1859, CHL.
15. Journal History, 10 October 1865, CHL.
16. Minutes and Festival Attendance, 1865–1867, Zion's Camp Festival Papers, 1863–1867, MS 14789, CHL.
17. Minutes and Festival Attendance, 1865–1867, CHL.
18. Matthew C. Godfrey, "'We Believe the Hand of the Lord Is in It': Memories of Divine Intervention in the Zion's Camp Expedition," *BYU Studies Quarterly* 56, no. 4 (2017): 105–106; David M. Wrobel, *Promised Lands: Promotion, Memory, and the Creation of the American West* (Lawrence: University Press of Kansas, 2002), 121–126.

NOTES

19. Journal History, 9 October 1869, CHL.
20. "The Zion's Camp Party," *Deseret Evening News*, 11 October 1869, 3.
21. "The Zion's Camp Party," *Deseret Evening News*, 3.
22. Jaques, letter to Young, 2 July 1870, CHL.
23. Jaques, letter to Young, 2 July 1870, CHL.
24. Jaques, letter to Young, 2 July 1870, CHL.
25. Journal History, 10 October 1865, CHL.

CHAPTER 15: RELIEF SOCIETY

1. Twelfth Ward, Salt Lake Stake, Relief Society Minutes and Records, 29 April 1868, 1–2, LR 12908 24, CHL.
2. Of teachers, Eliza R. Snow advised: "In making choice of teachers be very careful it is a position of great responsibility; I never felt myself fully qualified for that office. The teachers in visiting should not call merely to beg; though they should always accept the smallest offering. Choose the wisest women cannot obtain enough to fill such positions; these women must be filled with the Holy Ghost Know how to impart wise instructions suitable to the circumstances of individuals. Some are given to sorrow; you can warm them up as a mother does her infant by taking them to your bosoms. By doing the best you can you will increase." (Eleventh Ward, University West Stake, Relief Society Minutes, 3 March 1869, LR 2569 14, CHL, available online at https://www.churchhistorianspress.org/eliza-r-snow/1860s/1869/03/1869-03-03.)
3. Nauvoo Relief Society Minutes, 28 July 1843, 101; Jill Mulvay Derr, Carol Cornwall Madsen, Kate Holbrook, and Matthew J. Grow, eds., *The First Fifty Years of Relief Society: Key Documents in Latter-Day Saint Women's History* (Salt Lake City: Church Historian's Press, 2016), 110.
4. Eleventh Ward, Relief Society Minutes, 3 March 1869, CHL.
5. For more on the history of the Relief Society, see Derr, et al., *First Fifty Years*, 236–241; Jill Mulvay Derr, Janath Russell Cannon, and Maureen Ursenbach Beecher, *Women of Covenant: The Story of Relief Society* (Salt Lake City and Provo, UT: Deseret Book Company and Brigham Young University Press, 1992).
6. Derr, et al., *First Fifty Years*, 235, 237.
7. Derr, et al., *First Fifty Years*, 245.
8. Twelfth Ward, Relief Society Minutes, 5–7, 20–21, 49, 52–53, 61, 76, 86, 89, 103, 122, 140, 142, 145, 154, 165, 177, 197, 224, 261, and 264.
9. Twelfth Ward, Relief Society Minutes, 5, 19, 21, 32, 53, 79, 86, 89, 109, 113, 180, 193, 204, and 209.
10. Twelfth Ward, Relief Society Minutes, 127–128, 142, 156, and 195.
11. Vienna Jaques to Brigham Young, June 1874, in Brigham Young Family Collection, MS 33661, box 1, folder 1, CHL.
12. Twelfth Ward, Relief Society Minutes, 2 May and 4 June 1874, 184, 186, CHL; Eliza R. Snow, Discourse to the Salt Lake City Tenth Ward Relief Society and Young

NOTES

Ladies, 30 April 1874, available online at https://www.churchhistorianspress.org/eliza-r-snow/1870s/1874/04/1874-04-30.
13. Emmeline B. Wells, Journal, 13 January 1875, CHL, available at https://www.churchhistorianspress.org/emmeline-b-wells/1870s/1875/1875-01?lang=eng.
14. Twelfth Ward Relief Society, Record Book, 1868–1877, 4 March 1870, 54–55, and March 1874, 177, CHL.
15. Derr, et al., *First Fifty Years*, 239.
16. Twelfth Ward, Relief Society Minutes, 2 April 1874, 180–182, CHL. Records indicate that Snow did attend the inaugural meeting of the Young Ladies Retrenchment Society for the Twelfth Ward on 26 August 1875. (Young Ladies Retrenchment Society Minutes, 26 August 1875, Salt Lake Twelfth Ward Young Ladies Mutual Improvement Association Minute Book, 3–4, CHL.)
17. Twelfth Ward Relief Society, Record Book, 27 February 1869; 24 April 1869; 4 March 1870; 2 December 1875; and 1 June 1876, 21, 27, 54, 222, and 233.
18. Twelfth Ward Relief Society, Record Book, 5 March 1874, 177.
19. Twelfth Ward Relief Society, Record Book, 177.
20. Twelfth War Relief Society, Record Book, 2 March 1876, 230.
21. "Home Affairs," *Woman's Exponent* 7, no. 3 (1 July 1878): 21.
22. George Hamlin, "In Memoriam," *Woman's Exponent* 12, no. 19 (1 March 1884): 152.
23. Brigham Young, letter to Isaac Groo, 8 September 1876, Brigham Young Collection, Outgoing Correspondence, CHL.
24. Twelfth Ward Relief Society, Record Book, 233.
25. Vienna Jaques, letter to Brigham Young, 2 July 1870, Incoming Correspondence, Brigham Young Collection, CHL.
26. Jaques, letter to Young, 2 July 1870, CHL.
27. For more on Latter-day Saint temple consciousness, see Richard E. Bennett, "'Which is the Wisest Course?': The Transformation in Mormon Temple Consciousness, 1870–1898," *BYU Studies Quarterly* 52, no. 2 (2013): 5–43; and Richard E. Bennett, "'Line Upon Line, Precept Upon Precept': Reflections on the 1877 Commencement of the Performance of Endowments and Sealings for the Dead," *BYU Studies* 44, no. 3 (2005): 38–77.

CHAPTER 16: AT THE GROVE

1. L.P. Kirby, "Provo Stirred by Scandal in Depot Fight," *Salt Lake Herald*, 6 May 1908, 1–2.
2. Historical Department, Journal History of the Church, 8 June 1876, 1, CHL.
3. Kenneth L. Cannon II, "'One of the Bitterest Fights in Provo History': The Controversies Over Provo's Union Depot," *Utah Historical Quarterly* 78, no. 3 (2010).
4. Kirby, "Provo Stirred by Scandal," *Salt Lake Herald*, 1–2.
5. Sarah Harris Passey, *Biographies of Utah Pioneers: Of Camp Bonneville, Provo, Utah*

NOTES

(Provo, Utah: Daughters of Utah Pioneers, 1940), 259; "A Gay Excursion Party," *Deseret News*, 21 June 1876.
6. Passey, *Biographies of Utah Pioneers*, 255.
7. "A Gay Excursion Party," *Deseret News*.
8. "A Gay Excursion Party," *Deseret News*.
9. "A Gay Excursion Party," *Deseret News*.
10. "A Gay Excursion Party," *Deseret News*.
11. Lida Ball, "History of Daniel Graves's Park Gardens," in Passey, *Biographies of Utah Pioneers*, 259.
12. Passey, *Biographies of Utah Pioneers*, 252, 255.
13. "A Gay Excursion Party," *Deseret News*.
14. Brian D. Reeves, "Hoary-Headed Saints: The Aged in Nineteenth-Century Mormon Culture," Master's thesis, Brigham Young University (August 1987), 76.
15. "Original Old Folks Committee," M243.6 O44o, CHL; Reeves, "Hoary-Headed Saints," 10.
16. "Never to be Forgotten," *Woman's Exponent*, 1 June 1875, 5.
17. Derr, et al., *First Fifty Years of Relief Society*, 375.
18. "Never to Be Forgotten," *Woman's Exponent*, 5.
19. "A Novel Excursion," *Deseret News*, 19 May 1875, 9.
20. "A Novel Excursion," *Deseret News*, 9.
21. "A Gay Excursion Party," *Deseret News*.
22. "A Gay Excursion Party," *Deseret News*.
23. "A Gay Excursion Party," *Deseret News*; Wilford Woodruff, Journal, 8 June 1876, CHL; George Goddard, Journal, 8 June 1876, MS 2737, box 92, folder 2, CHL.
24. "A Gay Excursion Party," *Deseret News*.
25. Goddard, Journal, 8 June 1876, CHL.
26. "A Gay Excursion Party," *Deseret News*.
27. Goddard, Journal, 8 June 1876, CHL.
28. Goddard, Journal, 8–9 June 1876, CHL.
29. "A Gay Excursion Party," *Deseret News*.
30. Wilford Woodruff, Journal, 8 June 1876, CHL.
31. "Excursion for the Old Folks," *Woman's Exponent* 8, no. 3 (1 July 1879), 20.
32. "A Novel Excursion," *Deseret News*, 8.
33. "Original Old Folks Committee," CHL; Reeves, "Hoary-Headed Saints," 10.
31. Reeves, "Hoary-Headed Saints," 36.
32. "Old Folks' Excursion," *Deseret News*, 2 July 1879, 8; see also Justin R. Bray, "Silver Locks in Zion: Old Age, Elderhood, and the Latter-day Saints," (PhD Diss., University of Utah, 2020), 96–104.
33. Joseph Smith, Remarks, 14 May 1843, available at https://www.josephsmithpapers.org/paper-summary/remarks-14-may-1843-as-reported-by-wilford-woodruff/1.
34. Reeves, "Hoary-Headed Saints," 30–32.

NOTES

35. Proverbs 16:31.
36. Woodruff, Journal, 8 June 1876, CHL.
37. "Old Folks' Excursion," *Deseret News*, 8.
38. "Old Folks' Excursion," *Deseret News*, 8.
39. Vienna is listed as being 93 years old in the article, but she would have just turned 92 on 10 June 1879. "Old Folks' Excursion," *Deseret News*, 8.
40. "Old Folks' Excursion," *Deseret News*, 8.
41. "Old Folks' Excursion," *Deseret News*, 8.
42. "Old Folks' Excursion," *Deseret News*, 8.
43. "Old Folks' Excursion," *Deseret News*, 8.
44. "Home Affairs," *Woman's Exponent* 8, no. 2 (15 June 1879): 12.
45. "Home Affairs," *Woman's Exponent* 8, no. 2, 12.
46. Reeves, "Hoary-Headed Saints," 36.

CHAPTER 17: FINAL DAYS IN SALT LAKE CITY

1. Howland V. Stevenson, Salt Lake City 12th Ward, Salt Lake County, Utah, 8, Supervisor's District No. 136, Enumeration District No. 51, 2 June 1880.
2. Department of Interior, Census Office, Enumerator Instructions, 1 May 1880, 10.
3. "Birthday Anniversary of One of Our Oldest Veterans," *Woman's Exponent* 9, no. 2 (15 June 1880), 13.
4. "Birthday Anniversary," *Woman's Exponent*, 13.
5. "Home Affairs," *Woman's Exponent* 8, no. 2 (15 June 1879): 12; "Birthday Anniversary," *Woman's Exponent*, 13; "Birthday Anniversary," *Salt Lake Herald*, 13 June 1882.
6. "Local and Other Matters. From Friday's Daily, Dec. 24," *Deseret News*, 29 December 1880; "Anniversary Gathering," *Woman's Exponent* 9, no. 15 (1 January 1881): 116; "Mormon Veterans," *Deseret News*, 5 April 1882.
7. "Local and Other Matters," *Deseret News*; "Anniversary Gathering," *Woman's Exponent*.
8. To read these addresses, see General Joseph Smith's Appeal to the Green Mountain Boys, 21 November–circa 3 December 1843, available at https://www.josephsmithpapers.org/paper-summary/general-joseph-smiths-appeal-to-the-green-mountain-boys-21-november-circa-3-december-1843/1>; Discourse, 18 June 1844, available at https://www.josephsmithpapers.org/paper-summary/discourse-18-june-1844-as-reported-by-william-clayton/1.
9. "Local and Other Matters," *Deseret News*.
10. "Local and Other Matters," *Deseret News*.
11. Wilford Woodruff, Journal, 23 April 1881, CHL.
12. Case File, ACQ 20-3, Church History Museum.
13. Handbook Guide to the Salt Lake Museum, September 1881, CHL.

NOTES

14. Jennifer Reeder, "Eliza R. Snow and the Prophet's Gold Watch: Time Keeper as Relic," *Journal of Mormon History* 31, no. 1 (Spring 2005): 120, 122.
15. Wilford Woodruff, Journal, 19 May 1881, CHL.
16. 1870 Census, 12th Ward, Salt Lake City, Salt Lake County, Utah, 3.
17. Indenture, Vienna Jaques to Joseph F. Smith, 31 December 1881, Joseph F. Smith Papers, CHL.
18. Indenture, Jaques to Joseph F. Smith, CHL.
19. George Q. Cannon, Journal, 27 March 1887, CHL, available at https://www.churchhistorianspress.org/george-q-cannon/1880s/1887/03-1887.
20. "Home Affairs," *Woman's Exponent* 8, no. 2, 12; "Birthday Anniversary," *Woman's Exponent*, 13; "Birthday Anniversary," *Salt Lake Herald*.
21. "Birthday Anniversary," *Salt Lake Herald*.
22. "Birthday Anniversary," *Salt Lake Herald*.
23. "Vienna Jacques Dead," *Deseret News*, 13 February 1884; see also *Ogden Daily Herald*, 8 February 1884.
24. George Hamlin, "In Memoriam," *Woman's Exponent* 12, no. 19 (1 March 1884): 152; "Vienna Jacques Dead," *Deseret News*; "Funeral Services," *Deseret News*, 13 February 1884.

CHAPTER 18: LAID TO REST

1. "Vienna Jacques Dead," *Deseret News,* 13 February 1884; see also *Ogden Daily Herald*, 8 February 1884.
2. Wilford Woodruff, Journal, 10 February 1884, CHL.
3. "Funeral Services," *Deseret News*, 13 February 1884.
4. "Vienna Jacques Dead," *Deseret News*; see also *Ogden Daily Herald*, 8 February 1884.
5. Wilford Woodruff, Journal, 10 February 1884, CHL.
6. "Funeral Services," *Deseret News*.
7. George Hamlin, "In Memoriam," *Woman's Exponent* 12, no. 19 (1 March 1884): 152.
8. Hamlin, "In Memoriam," 152.
9. "Home Affairs," *Woman's Exponent* 7, no. 3 (1 July 1878): 21; "Funeral Services," *Deseret News*.

POSTLUDE

1. See Brent M. Rogers, "The Fascinating Life of Vienna Jaques," *Mormon Historical Studies* 16, no. 1 (Spring 2015): 148–178; and Brent M. Rogers, "Vienna Jaques: Woman of Faith," *Ensign* (June 2016): 40–45.

Bibliography

ARCHIVAL SOURCES AND COLLECTIONS

BYU—L. Tom Perry Special Collections, Harold B. Lee Library, Brigham Young University, Provo, Utah

    Holbrook, Joseph. "The Life of Joseph Holbrook, 1806–1871." Typescript.

CCLA—Community of Christ Library and Archives, Independence, Missouri

    Scott, Jacob. Letter to Mary Scott Warnock. January 5, 1844.

CHL—Church History Library, The Church of Jesus Christ of Latter-day Saints, Salt Lake City, Utah

    1850 Utah Territorial Census, Salt Lake County.
    1870 Census, Twelfth Ward, Salt Lake City, Salt Lake County, Utah.
    1880 Census, Utah Territory, Salt Lake County.
    Ames, Ira. Autobiography.
    Cannon, George Q. Journal.
    Chase, Sherwin. Information Concerning Daniel Shearer, circa 1983.
    Cowdery, Oliver. Letterbook.
    Department of Interior, Census Office. Enumerator Instructions, May 1, 1880.
    Eleventh Ward, University West Stake. Relief Society Minutes.
    Far West and Nauvoo Elders' Certificates, 1837–1846.
    Far West Committee Minutes, January–April 1839.
    Female Council of Health. Minutes.
    Goddard, George. Journal.

BIBLIOGRAPHY

Handbook Guide to the Salt Lake Museum, September 1881.
Historical Department, Journal History of the Church.
Hyde, Orson. Journal.
Jacobs, Zina Huntington. Diary.
Johnson, Benjamin F. Reminiscences and Journal.
Joseph Smith Papers, Revelations Collection.
Kimball, Vilate Murray. Letters, 1840.
Knight, Newel. Autobiography and Journal.
Manuscript History of the Church, vol. A-1.
Millet, Artemus. Reminiscences.
Noble, Joseph B. Reminiscences.
"Original Old Folks Committee," Broadside.
Partridge, Edward. Papers.
Phelps, William W. Collection of Missouri Documents.
Porter, Nathan T. Reminiscences, ca. 1879.
Relief Society Minutebook, March 1842–March 1844.
Rich, Emeline Grover. Autobiography and Diary.
Rich, Charles C. Journal.
Rich, Mary Ann Phelps. Autobiography.
Richards, Willard. Journals and Papers, 1821–1854.
Sessions, Patty. Diary.
Smith, Hyrum. Diary.
Smith, Joseph. Collection.
Smith, Joseph. History Documents, 1839–1860.
Smith, Joseph F. Papers.
Smith, Lucy Mack. History, 1844–1845, bk. 14.
Smith, Samuel Harrison. Diary.
Twelfth Ward, Salt Lake Stake. Relief Society Minutes and Records.
Twelfth Ward, Salt Lake Stake. Young Ladies Mutual Improvement Association Minute Book.
Van Buren, Martin. Correspondence, 1839–1844.
Wells, Emmeline B. Journal.
Whitney, Helen Mar Kimball. Autobiography.
Woodruff, Wilford. Collection.
Young, Brigham. Collection.
Young, Brigham. Family Collection.
Young, Lorenzo D. Papers.
Zion's Camp Festival. Papers, 1863–1867.

FHL—Family History Library, The Church of Jesus Christ of Latter-day Saints, Salt Lake City, Utah

BIBLIOGRAPHY

State Archives, Boston, microfilm 960,179, U.S. and Canada Records Collection.
The Church of Jesus Christ of Latter-day Saints, Salt Lake City 12th Ward, Salt Lake City, Salt Lake Co., UT, Record of Members, [1849]–1941, 11, microfilm 26,723, U.S. and Canada Records Collection.

MHS—Massachusetts Historical Society, Boston, Massachusetts
Storrow, Thomas Wentworth. "Journey to the West," no date. Storrow Family Papers, 1762–1999.

MLSC—J. Willard Marriott Library, Special Collections, University of Utah, Salt Lake City, Utah
Brodie, Fawn McKay. Papers.
Crawford, Vesta P. Papers.
Durham, Reed C. Papers.
Newell, Linda King. Collection.
Noall, Matthew Frederick and Claire Wilcox. Papers.
Sanborn, Daniel A. "Salt Lake City, 1889: Sheet 034," Sanborn Map Collection, available at https://collections.lib.utah.edu/ark:/87278/s6dn4g8p.

NARA—National Archives and Records Administration, Washington, DC
Records of the United States Senate, 26th–28th Congress, RG 46, Box 91.

NEWSPAPERS AND PERIODICALS

American Traveller (Boston)
Boston Courier
Christian Register (Boston)
Cincinnati Journal
Deseret News (Salt Lake City)
Eastern Argus (Portland, Maine)
Kansas City [MO] *Daily Journal*
Latter Day Saints' Messenger and Advocate (Kirtland, Ohio)
Millennial Star (Liverpool)
Missouri Republican (St. Louis)
New York Morning Herald
New York Spectator
New York Tribune
Niles' Weekly Register (Baltimore)
Ogden [UT] *Daily Herald*
Ohio Observer (Hudson)
Quincy [IL] *Whig*
Salem [MA] *Gazette*
Salt Lake Herald

BIBLIOGRAPHY

The Evening and the Morning Star (Independence, Missouri, and Kirtland, Ohio)
The Saints' Herald (Independence, Missouri)
Times and Seasons (Nauvoo, Illinois)
Warsaw [IL] *Signal*
Woman's Exponent (Salt Lake City)

BOOKS AND ARTICLES

Allison, Christopher M.B. "Layered Lives: Boston Mormons and the Spatial Contexts of Conversion." *Journal of Mormon History* 42, no. 2 (April 2016): 168–213.

Anderson, Lavina Fielding. "Ministering Angels: Single Women in Mormon Society." *Dialogue* 16, no. 3 (Fall 1983): 59–72.

Arrington, Leonard J. *Charles C. Rich*. Provo, UT: Brigham Young University Press, 1974.

———. *Great Basin Kingdom: An Economic History of the Latter-day Saints, 1830–1900*. Reprint edition. Salt Lake City: University of Utah Press, 1993.

Arrington, Leonard J., and Susan Arrington Madsen. *Sunbonnet Sisters: True Stories of Mormon Women and Frontier Life*. Salt Lake City: Bookcraft, 1984.

Austin, Emily M. *Mormonism; or, Life among the Mormons: Being an Autobiographical Sketch; Including an Experience of Fourteen Years of Mormon Life*. Madison, WI: M.J. Cantwell, 1882.

Baugh, Alexander L. "'For This Ordinance Belongeth to My House': The Practice of Baptism for the Dead Outside the Nauvoo Temple." *Mormon Historical Studies* 3, no. 1 (Spring 2002): 47–58.

Beecher, Maureen Ursenbach, ed. *The Personal Writings of Eliza Roxcy Snow*. Logan: Utah State University Press, 2000.

Bennett, Richard E. "'Line Upon Line, Precept Upon Precept': Reflections on the 1877 Commencement of the Performance of Endowments and Sealings for the Dead." *BYU Studies* 44, no. 3 (2005): 38–77.

———. *Mormons at the Missouri: Winter Quarters, 1846–1852*. Norman: University of Oklahoma Press, 2004.

———. "'Which is the Wisest Course?': The Transformation in Mormon Temple Consciousness, 1870–1898." *BYU Studies Quarterly* 52, no. 2 (2013): 5–43.

Bishop, M. Guy. "'What Has Become of Our Fathers?': Baptism for the Dead at Nauvoo." *Dialogue: A Journal of Mormon Thought* 23, no. 2 (Summer 1990): 85–97.

Black, Susan Easton. "Happiness in Womanhood." *Ensign* (March 2002).

Black, Susan Easton, and Harvey Bischoff Black, eds. *Annotated Record of Baptisms for the Dead, 1840–1845: Nauvoo, Hancock County, Illinois*, Volume 5. Provo, UT: Center for Family History and Genealogy, Brigham Young University, 2002.

Black, Susan Easton, and Mary Jane Woodger. *Women of Character: Profiles of 100 Prominent LDS Women*. American Fork, UT: Covenant Communications, 2011.

Bray, Justin R. "Silver Locks in Zion: Old Age, Elderhood, and the Latter-day Saints." PhD Diss., University of Utah, 2020.

BIBLIOGRAPHY

Brodie, Fawn M. *No Man Knows My History: The Life of Joseph Smith, Mormon Prophet.* New York: Alfred A. Knopf, 1990, second edition.

Bryant, Laurie J. *A Modest Homestead: Life in Small Adobe Homes in Salt Lake City, 1850–1897.* Salt Lake City: University of Utah Press, 2017.

Bushman, Richard Lyman. *Joseph Smith: Rough Stone Rolling.* New York: Alfred A. Knopf, 2005.

Cannon II, Kenneth L. "'One of the Bitterest Fights in Provo History': The Controversies Over Provo's Union Depot." *Utah Historical Quarterly* 78, no. 3 (2010): 230–253.

Carvalho, Solomon Nunes. *Incidents of Travel and Adventure in the Far West with Colonel Fremont's Last Expedition.* Lincoln: University of Nebraska Press, 2004.

Chester, Joseph Lemuel. *John Rogers: The Compiler of the First Authorised English Bible.* London: Longman, Green, Longman, and Roberts, 1861.

Compton, Todd. "A Trajectory of Plurality: An Overview of Joseph Smith's Thirty-three Plural Wives." *Dialogue: A Journal of Mormon Thought* 29, no. 2 (Summer 1996): 1–38.

———. "Fawn Brodie on Joseph Smith's Plural Wives and Polygamy: A Critical View." In Newell G. Bringhurst, ed. *Reconsidering No Man Knows My History: Fawn Brodie and Joseph Smith in Retrospect.* Logan: Utah State University Press, 1996.

———. *In Sacred Loneliness: The Plural Wives of Joseph Smith.* Salt Lake City: Signature Books, 1997.

Cott, Nancy F. *The Bonds of Womanhood: "Woman's Sphere" in New England, 1780–1835.* New Haven, CT: Yale University Press, 1977.

Daughters of Utah Pioneers. *Pioneer Women of Faith and Fortitude*, Vol. 4. Salt Lake City: International Daughters of Utah Pioneers and Publishers Press, 1998.

Department of Commerce and Labor, Bureau of the Census, S.N.D. North, Director. *Heads of Families at the First Census of the United States taken in the Year 1790: Massachusetts.* Washington: Government Printing Office, 1908.

Derr, Jill Mulvay, Carol Cornwall Madsen, Kate Holbrook, and Matthew J. Grow, eds. *The First Fifty Years of Relief Society: Key Documents in Latter-Day Saint Women's History.* Salt Lake City: Church Historian's Press, 2016.

Derr, Jill Mulvay, Janath Russell Cannon, and Maureen Ursenbach Beecher. *Women of Covenant: The Story of Relief Society.* Salt Lake City and Provo, UT: Deseret Book Company and Brigham Young University Press, 1992.

Dinger, Steven C. "'The Doctors in This Region Don't Know Much': Medicine and Obstetrics in Mormon Nauvoo." *Journal of Mormon History* 42, no. 4 (October 2016): 51–68.

Esplin, Ronald K., Dean C. Jessee, Brent M. Rogers, Gerrit J. Dirkmaat, and Andrew H. Hedges, eds. *The Brigham Young Journals, Volume 1: April 1832–February 1846.* Provo, UT: Brigham Young University Press, 2023.

Faulring, Scott H., Kent P. Jackson, and Robert J. Matthews, eds. *Joseph Smith's New*

BIBLIOGRAPHY

Translation of the Bible: Original Manuscripts. Provo, UT: Religious Studies Center, Brigham Young University, 2004.

Ferris, Mrs. B.G. (Elizabeth). *The Mormons at Home; With some Incidents of Travel from Missouri to California, 1852–3.* New York: Dix & Edwards, 1856.

Fielding, Robert Kent. "The Growth of the Mormon Church in Kirtland, Ohio." PhD Diss., Indiana University, 1957.

Frederickson, Kristine Wardle. *Extraordinary Courage: Women Empowered by the Gospel of Jesus Christ.* Salt Lake City: Eagle Gate, 2013.

Glaeser, Edward L. "Reinventing Boston: 1640–2003." Working Paper 10166, NBER Working Paper Series, National Bureau of Economic Research, Cambridge, MA: December 2003.

Godfrey, Kenneth W., Audrey M. Godfrey, and Jill Mulvay Derr. *Women's Voices: An Untold History of the Latter-day Saints, 1830–1900.* Salt Lake City: Deseret Book Company, 1982.

Godfrey, Matthew C. "'The Redemption of Zion Must Needs Come by Power': Insights into the Camp of Israel Expedition, 1834." *BYU Studies Quarterly* 53, no. 4 (2014): 125–146.

———. "'We Believe the Hand of the Lord Is in It': Memories of Divine Intervention in the Zion's Camp Expedition." *BYU Studies Quarterly* 56, no. 4 (2017): 99–132.

———. "Wise Men and Wise Women: The Role of Church Members in Financing Church Operations, 1834–1835." *Journal of Mormon History* 43, no. 3 (2017): 1–21.

Hales, Brian C. "Fanny Alger and Joseph Smith's Pre-Nauvoo Reputation." *Journal of Mormon History* 35, no. 4 (Fall 2009): 112–190.

Hales, Brian C., and Gregory L. Smith. "A Response to Grant Palmer's 'Sexual Allegations against Joseph Smith and the Beginnings of Polygamy in Nauvoo.'" *Interpreter: A Journal of Mormon Scripture* 12 (2014): 183–236.

Hamlin, George. "In Memoriam." *Woman's Exponent* 12, no. 19 (March 1, 1884): 152.

Hartley, William G. "'Almost Too Intolerable a Burthen': The Winter Exodus from Missouri, 1838–39." *Journal of Mormon History* 18 (Fall 1992): 6–40.

Hascall, Ursalia B. Hastings to Col. Wilson Andrews, 19 September 1846, in *The Nauvoo Journal*, Vol. 5, No. 1 (Spring 1993):13.

Hill, Jennifer J. *Birthing the West: Mothers and Midwives in the Rockies and Plains.* Lincoln: University of Nebraska Press, 2022.

Hurd, Duane Hamilton. *History of Essex County, Massachusetts.* Philadelphia: J.W. Lewis & Co., 1888.

International Society Daughters of Utah Pioneers. *Pioneer Women of Faith and Fortitude* 4 vols. Salt Lake City: Publishers Press, 1998.

Jennings, Warren A. "The Army of Israel Marches into Missouri." *Missouri Historical Review* 62, no. 2 (January 1968): 107–135.

BIBLIOGRAPHY

Jensen, Robin Scott. "'Archives of the Better World': The Nineteenth-Century Historian's Office and Mormonism's Archival Flexibility." PhD Diss., University of Utah, 2019.

Jenson, Andrew. *Latter-day Saint Biographical Encyclopedia.* Vol. 1. Salt Lake City: Andrew Jenson History Company and Deseret News Press, 1901.

Johnson, Clark V., ed. *Mormon Redress Petitions: Documents of the 1833–1838 Missouri Conflict.* Provo, UT: Religious Studies Center, Brigham Young University, 1992.

Johnson, Janiece, and Jennifer Reeder. *The Witness of Women: Firsthand Experiences and Testimonies from the Restoration.* Salt Lake City: Deseret Book, 2016.

Jones, Dan. "The Martyrdom of Joseph Smith and His Brother Hyrum." Introduced by Ronald D. Dennis, in *BYU Studies Quarterly* 24, no. 1 (1984): 79–109.

Jortner, Adam. "'Some Little Necromancy': Politics, Religion, and the Mormons, 1829–1838." In Spencer W. McBride, Brent M. Rogers, and Keith A. Erekson, eds., *Contingent Citizens: Shifting Perceptions of Latter-day Saints in American Political Culture.* Ithaca, NY: Cornell University Press, 2020.

JSP, D1—Michael Hubbard MacKay, Gerrit J. Dirkmaat, Grant Underwood, Robert J. Woodford, and William G. Hartley, eds. *The Joseph Smith Papers, Documents, Volume 1: July 1828–June 1831.* Salt Lake City: Church Historian's Press, 2013.

JSP, D2—Matthew C. Godfrey, Mark Ashurst-McGee, Grant Underwood, Robert J. Woodford, and William G. Hartley, eds. *The Joseph Smith Papers, Documents, Volume 2: July 1831–January 1833.* Salt Lake City: Church Historian's Press, 2013.

JSP, D3—Gerrit J. Dirkmaat, Brent M. Rogers, Grant Underwood, Robert J. Woodford, and William G. Hartley, eds. *The Joseph Smith Papers, Documents, Volume 3: February 1833–March 1834.* Salt Lake City: Church Historian's Press, 2014.

JSP, D5—Brent M. Rogers, Elizabeth A. Kuehn, Christian K. Heimburger, Max H Parkin, Alexander L. Baugh, and Steven C. Harper, eds. *The Joseph Smith Papers, Documents, Volume 5: October 1835–January 1838.* Salt Lake City: Church Historian's Press, 2017.

JSP, D6—Mark Ashurst-McGee, David W. Grua, Elizabeth A. Kuehn, Brenden W. Rensink, and Alexander L. Baugh, eds. *The Joseph Smith Papers, Documents, Volume 6: February 1838–August 1839.* Salt Lake City: Church Historian's Press, 2017.

JSP, D7—Matthew C. Godfrey, Spencer W. McBride, Alex D. Smith, and Christopher James Blythe, eds. *The Joseph Smith Papers, Documents, Volume 7: September 1839–January 1841.* Salt Lake City: Church Historian's Press, 2018.

JSP, D8—Brent M. Rogers, Mason K. Allred, Gerrit J. Dirkmaat, and Brett D. Dowdle, eds. *The Joseph Smith Papers, Documents, Volume 8: February–November 1841.* Salt Lake City: Church Historian's Press, 2019.

JSP, D12—David W. Grua, Brent M. Rogers, Matthew C. Godfrey, Robin Scott Jensen, Christopher James Blythe, and Jessica M. Nelson, eds. *The Joseph Smith Papers, Documents, Volume 12: March–July 1843.* Salt Lake City: Church Historian's Press, 2019.

BIBLIOGRAPHY

JSP, H2—Karen Lynn Davidson, Richard L. Jensen, and David J. Whitaker, eds. *Histories 2, Assigned Histories, 1831–1847*. Salt Lake City: Church Historian's Press, 2012.

JSP, J1—Dean C. Jessee, Mark Ashurst-McGee, and Richard L. Jensen, eds. *The Joseph Smith Papers, Journals, Volume 1: 1832–1839*. Salt Lake City: Church Historian's Press, 2008.

JSP, J2—Andrew H. Hedges, Alex D. Smith, and Richard Lloyd Anderson, eds. *The Joseph Smith Papers, Journals, Volume 2: December 1841–April 1843*. Salt Lake City: Church Historian's Press, 2011.

JSP, J3—Andrew H. Hedges, Alex D. Smith, and Brent M. Rogers, eds. *The Joseph Smith Papers, Journals, Volume 3: May 1843–June 1844*. Salt Lake City: Church Historian's Press, 2015.

JSP, R1—Robin Scott Jensen, Robert J. Woodford, and Brent M. Rogers, eds. *The Joseph Smith Papers, Revelations and Translations, Volume 1: Manuscript Revelation Books*. Salt Lake City: Church Historian's Press.

JSP, R2—Robin Scott Jensen, Richard E. Turley Jr., Riley M. Lorimer, eds. *The Joseph Smith Papers, Revelations and Translations, Volume 2: Published Revelations*. Salt Lake City: Church Historian's Press, 2012.

Kennedy, Lawrence W. *Planning the City Upon a Hill: Boston Since 1630*. Amherst: University of Massachusetts Press, 1992.

Kerber, Linda K. "A Constitutional Right to be Treated like American Ladies: Women and the Obligations of Citizenship." In Linda K. Kerber, Alice Kessler-Harris, and Kathryn Kish Sklar, eds. *U. S. History as Women's History: New Feminist Essays*. Chapel Hill: University of North Carolina Press, 1995.

Launius, Roger D. *The Kirtland Temple: A Historical Narrative*. Independence, MO: Herald Publishing House, 1986.

Littlefield, Lyman Omer. *Reminiscences of Latter-day Saints*. Logan, UT: The Utah Journal Co., 1888.

McCaughey, Robert A. "From Town to City: Boston in the 1820s." *Political Science Quarterly* 88, no. 2 (June 1973): 191–213.

McMahon, Billy J. "'Humane and Considerate Attention': Indian Removal from Missouri, 1803–1838," Master's Thesis, Northwest Missouri State University, 2013.

Morison, Samuel E. *The Maritime History of Massachusetts*. Boston: Northeastern University Press, 1961.

Neyman, Jane H. "Be Forbearing and Forgiving," 4 November 1869. Jennifer Reeder and Kate Holbrook, eds. *At the Pulpit: 185 Years of Discourses by Latter-day Saint Women*. Salt Lake City: Church Historian's Press, 2017.

Passey, Sarah Harris. *Biographies of Utah Pioneers: Of Camp Bonneville, Provo, Utah*. Provo, UT: Daughters of Utah Pioneers, 1940.

Peterson, Paul H. "An Historical Analysis of the Word of Wisdom." Master's thesis, Brigham Young University, 1972.

BIBLIOGRAPHY

Peterson, Paul H., and Ronald W. Walker. "Brigham Young's Word of Wisdom Legacy." *BYU Studies* 42, nos. 3 & 4 (2003): 29–64.

Poll, Richard D. "The Move South." *BYU Studies* 29, no. 4 (1989): 65–88.

Pratt, Parley P. *History of the Late Persecution Inflicted by the State of Missouri upon the Mormons.* Detroit: Dawson and Bates, 1839.

Radke, Andrea G. "We Also Marched: The Women and Children of Zion's Camp, 1834." *BYU Studies* 39, no. 1 (2000): 147–165.

Reeder, Jennifer. "Eliza R. Snow and the Prophet's Gold Watch: Time Keeper as Relic." *Journal of Mormon History* 31, no. 1 (Spring 2005): 119–141.

Reeves, Brian D. "Hoary-Headed Saints: The Aged in Nineteenth-Century Mormon Culture." Master's thesis, Brigham Young University, August 1987.

Robison, Elwin C. *The First Mormon Temple: Design, Construction, and Historic Context of the Kirtland Temple.* Provo, UT: Brigham Young University Press, 1997.

Rogers, Brent M. "To the 'Honest and Patriotic Sons of Liberty': Mormon Appeals for Redress and Social Justice, 1843–44." *Journal of Mormon History* 39, no. 1 (Winter 2013): 36–67.

———. "The Fascinating Life of Vienna Jaques." *Mormon Historical Studies* 16, no. 1 (Spring 2015): 148–178.

———. Vienna Jaques: Woman of Faith." *Ensign* (June 2016): 40–45.

———. *Unpopular Sovereignty: Mormons and the Federal Management of Early Utah Territory.* Lincoln: University of Nebraska Press, 2017.

Salmon, Marylynn. *Women and the Law of Property in Early America.* Chapel Hill: University of North Carolina Press, 1986.

Smith III, Joseph. *Memoirs of President Joseph Smith III.* Independence, MO: Price Publishing, 2001.

Staker, Mark Lyman. *Hearken, O Ye People: The Historical Setting of Joseph Smith's Ohio Revelations.* Salt Lake City: Greg Kofford Books, 2009.

Stenhouse, Fanny. *Tell it All: The Story of a Life's Experience in Mormonism.* Hartford, CT: A. D. Worthington, 1875.

Stevenson, Howland V. Salt Lake City 12th Ward, Salt Lake County, Utah. Supervisor's District No. 136, Enumeration District No. 51, 2 June 1880.

Temin, Peter. *Engines of Enterprise: An Economic History of New England.* Cambridge, MA: Harvard University Press, 2000.

Temple Records Index Bureau. *Nauvoo Temple Endowment Register: 10 December 1845 to 8 February 1846.* Salt Lake City: The Church of Jesus Christ of Latter-day Saints, 1974.

The Boston Directory; Containing Names of the Inhabitants; Their Occupations, Places of Business and Dwelling Houses. Boston: John H. A. Frost, 1827, and Charles Stimpson, Jr., 1829.

The Church of Jesus Christ of Latter-day Saints. *Saints: The Story of The Church of Jesus*

BIBLIOGRAPHY

Christ in the Latter Days, Volume 1: The Standard of Truth, 1815–1846. Salt Lake City: The Church of Jesus Christ of Latter-day Saints, 2018.

Tobler, Ryan C. "'Saviors on Mount Zion': Mormon Sacramentalism, Mortality, and the Baptism for the Dead." *Journal of Mormon History* 39 (2013): 182–238.

Tullidge, Edward W. *History of Salt Lake City.* Salt Lake City: Star Printing Company, 1886.

———. *The Women of Mormondom.* New York: Tullidge and Crandall, 1877.

Turner, John G. *Brigham Young: Pioneer Prophet.* Cambridge, MA: The Belknap Press of Harvard University Press, 2012.

Ulrich, Laurel Thatcher. *A House Full of Females: Plural Marriage and Women's Rights in Early Mormonism, 1835–1870.* New York: Alfred A. Knopf, 2017.

———. *A Midwife's Tale: The Life of Martha Ballard, Based on Her Diary, 1785–1812.* New York: Vintage Books, 1991.

———. "Runaway Wives, 1830–1860." *Journal of Mormon History* 42, no. 2 (April 2016): 1–26.

———. *The Age of Homespun: Objects and Stories in the Creation of an American Myth.* New York: Alfred A. Knopf, 2001.

Van Orden, Bruce A. "Zion's Camp: A Refiner's Fire." In Larry C. Porter and Susan Easton Black, eds. *The Prophet Joseph: Essays on the Life and Mission of Joseph Smith.* Salt Lake City: Deseret Book, 1988, 192–207.

Vogel, Dan, ed. *History of Joseph Smith and The Church of Jesus Christ of Latter-day Saints: A Source and Text-Critical Edition, Volume 1: 1805–1833.* Salt Lake City: The Smith-Petit Foundation, 2015.

Walker, Ronald W., Richard E. Turley Jr., and Glen M. Leonard. *Massacre at Mountain Meadows.* New York: Oxford University Press, 2008.

Ward, Maurine Carr, ed. *Winter Quarters: The 1846–1848 Life Writings of Mary Haskin Parker Richards.* Logan: Utah State University Press, 1996.

Winslow, Brady G. "Vienna Jacques: Eyewitness to the Jackson County Persecutions." *Mormon Historical Studies* 11, no. 2 (Fall 2010): 93–98.

Wrobel, David M. *Promised Lands: Promotion, Memory, and the Creation of the American West.* Lawrence: University Press of Kansas, 2002.

Image Credits

Page 2: Vienna Jaques. Photograph by Edward Martin, circa 1867. Courtesy of the Church History Library, The Church of Jesus Christ of Latter-day Saints, Salt Lake City.

Page 24: Book of Mormon owned by Vienna Jaques. Photograph taken by Alex D. Smith, June 2024. Used with permission of photographer.

Page 30: Mobbers raiding printing office. Photograph of painting collected by Charles Brent Hancock. Photograph taken by Rinehart and Co., circa 1895. Courtesy of the Church History Library, The Church of Jesus Christ of Latter-day Saints, Salt Lake City.

Page 78: Nauvoo on the Mississippi River. Illustration by Hermann J. Meyer, New York, circa 1855. Courtesy of Library of Congress, Washington DC.

Page 91: Vienna Jaques letter to Brigham Young Vienna Jaques letter to Brigham Young, September 11, 1855. Courtesy of the Church History Library, The Church of Jesus Christ of Latter-day Saints, Salt Lake City.

Page 112: Salt Lake City looking east along South Temple Street. Savage and Ottinger Photography Studio, circa 1867. Courtesy of the Church History Library, The Church of Jesus Christ of Latter-day Saints, Salt Lake City.

Discussion Questions

1. Vienna Jaques is one of the few women mentioned by name in the Doctrine and Covenants. How does learning about her life and contributions change or expand your understanding of the role of women in early Church history? What lessons can modern Latter-day Saint women and men draw from her story?
2. Much of what we know about Vienna Jaques has been deduced from what little remains of her physical records, including the letters she sent and received. Think about the record you are keeping of your own life. What might your journals, texts, emails, and social media accounts reveal about who you are? Is there anything you'd like to change about your own personal record and how it reflects who you are and what you value?
3. Vienna's financial donations to the Church played a key role in its early survival. How does her example of generosity and sacrifice encourage you to consider your own relationship with giving—whether in time, talents, or resources? In what ways has giving strengthened you?
4. Vienna Jaques was present for many significant moments in Church

DISCUSSION QUESTIONS

history, from the establishment of the Relief Society to the early temple ordinances. What significant moments in the Church have you witnessed, and how has being part of them made you feel? When we need to build our faith in things we haven't personally experienced, what can we do to strengthen the spiritual gift named in Doctrine and Covenants 46:14, "to believe on [others'] words"?

5. Vienna endured trying times, including persecution in Missouri and painful personal losses. What can we learn from her resilience and faith in the face of trials? How might her example guide you in navigating your own challenges?

6. Throughout her life, Vienna made significant sacrifices and took great risks for her faith, especially on the journey to Utah. What uncertainties or adversities are you currently facing, and how can Vienna's example inspire you to approach your own difficulties?

7. As a member of the early Relief Society, Vienna contributed to the welfare of others. In what ways do you feel called to serve in the Church or your community today? How does Vienna's legacy inspire you to make a difference in the lives of those around you? What is one thing you might do today to be a better member of your own community?

8. Vienna Jaques remained unmarried throughout much of her life but found a deep sense of purpose and community within the Church. What can modern Latter-day Saint readers, both single and married, learn from her example about finding strength and fulfillment in the gospel? How might we all be better at reaching out to and making space for those who, for whatever reason, feel they don't "fit the mold"?

9. Vienna Jaques lived a simple life yet made profound contributions to the growth of the Church. How can her example of quiet faithfulness inspire you in your own discipleship? How have small acts of faith

and dedication affected your own life, and what can you do this week to strengthen your own habits of quiet discipleship?
10. Vienna Jaques's life reminds us that not all significant contributions to Church history are widely known. Who are some lesser-known figures in your own family or community whose stories inspire you? How can we better honor and remember those whose quiet faith has strengthened the Church?